First World War
and Army of Occupation
War Diary
France, Belgium and Germany

47 DIVISION
142 Infantry Brigade
London Regiment
23rd (County of London) Battalion
14 March 1915 - 3 May 1919

WO95/2744/1

The Naval & Military Press Ltd
www.nmarchive.com
Published in association with The National Archives

Published by

The Naval & Military Press Ltd

Unit 10 Ridgewood Industrial Park,

Uckfield, East Sussex,

TN22 5QE England

Tel: +44 (0) 1825 749494

www.naval-military-press.com

www.nmarchive.com

This diary has been reprinted in facsimile from the original. Any imperfections are inevitably reproduced and the quality may fall short of modern type and cartographic standards.

© Crown Copyright
Images reproduced by permission of The National Archives, London, England, 2015.

Contents

Document type	Place/Title	Date From	Date To
Heading	WO95/2744 Mar 15-Apr 19 1/23 London Regt		
Heading	47th Division 142nd Infy Bde 1-23rd London Regt March 1915-Apr 1919		
Heading	142nd Inf. Bde 47th Division 1/23rd London Regt March 1915 (14.3.15-31.3.15)		
War Diary	Albans	14/03/1915	14/03/1915
War Diary	Havre	15/03/1915	15/03/1915
War Diary	Rest Camp	16/03/1915	16/03/1915
War Diary	Arques	17/03/1915	19/03/1915
War Diary	Lespesses	20/03/1915	20/03/1915
War Diary	St Hilaire	21/03/1915	27/03/1915
War Diary	Labeuvriere	28/03/1915	31/03/1915
Heading	142nd Inf. Bde 47th Division 1/23rd London Regt April 1915		
War Diary	Labeuvriere	01/04/1915	08/04/1915
War Diary	Oblinghem	09/04/1915	11/04/1915
War Diary	Les Glaugmes	11/04/1915	19/04/1915
War Diary	Mesplaux	20/04/1915	20/04/1915
War Diary	Allouagne	21/04/1915	23/04/1915
War Diary	Les Choquaux	24/04/1915	24/04/1915
War Diary	Rue Du Bois	25/04/1915	28/04/1915
War Diary	Le Touret	29/04/1915	30/04/1915
Heading	142nd Inf. Bde 47th Division 1/23rd London Regt May 1915		
War Diary	Le Touret	01/05/1915	03/05/1915
War Diary	Rue Du Bois	04/05/1915	06/05/1915
War Diary	Le Preol	07/05/1915	14/05/1915
War Diary	Cuinchy	17/05/1915	17/05/1915
War Diary	Tourbieres	18/05/1915	20/05/1915
War Diary	Cuinchy	21/05/1915	21/05/1915
War Diary	Beuvry	22/05/1915	24/05/1915
War Diary	Givenchy	25/05/1915	26/05/1915
War Diary	Le Quesnol	27/05/1915	31/05/1915
Heading	Appendix I		
Miscellaneous	Report On Operation May 25-26 1915	28/05/1915	28/05/1915
Heading	142nd Inf. Bde 47th Division 1/23rd London Regt June 1915		
War Diary	Le Quesnol	01/06/1915	14/06/1915
War Diary	Maroc	15/06/1915	17/06/1915
War Diary	Les Brebis	18/06/1915	20/06/1915
War Diary	Noeux Les Mines	21/06/1915	28/06/1915
War Diary	Section X2	29/06/1915	29/06/1915
Heading	142nd Inf. Bde 47th Division 1/23rd London Regt July 1915		
War Diary	Section X2	01/07/1915	14/07/1915
War Diary	Mazingarbe	15/07/1915	23/07/1915
War Diary	Section W.3	24/07/1915	31/07/1915
Heading	142nd Inf. Bde 47th Division 1/23rd London Regt August 1915		
War Diary	Section W.3	01/08/1915	02/08/1915

War Diary	Houchain	03/08/1915	03/08/1915
War Diary	Lozinghem	04/08/1915	11/08/1915
War Diary	Noeux Les Mines	12/08/1915	18/08/1915
War Diary	Allouagne	19/08/1915	31/08/1915
Heading	142nd Bde 47th Division 1/23rd London Regiment September 1915		
War Diary	Les Brebis	01/09/1915	03/09/1915
War Diary	Sector W.3	04/09/1915	23/09/1915
War Diary	Les Brebis	24/09/1915	27/09/1915
War Diary	Loos	28/09/1915	30/09/1915
Heading	142nd Inf. Bde 47th Division 1/23rd London Regt October 1915		
War Diary	Loos	01/10/1915	01/10/1915
War Diary	Les Brebis	02/10/1915	02/10/1915
War Diary	Fouquieres	03/10/1915	06/10/1915
War Diary	Noeux Les Mines	07/10/1915	12/10/1915
War Diary	Trenches	13/10/1915	20/10/1915
War Diary	Philosophe	21/10/1915	23/10/1915
War Diary	Section B.2	24/10/1915	31/10/1915
Heading	142nd Inf Bde 47th Division 1/23rd London Regt November 1915		
War Diary	Section B2	01/11/1915	06/11/1915
War Diary	Philosophe	07/11/1915	13/11/1915
War Diary	Lozinghem	14/11/1915	30/11/1915
Heading	142nd Inf. Bde 47th Division 1/23rd London Regt December 1915		
War Diary	Lozinghem	01/12/1915	14/12/1915
War Diary	Vaudricourt	15/12/1915	15/12/1915
War Diary	D.1	16/12/1915	23/12/1915
War Diary	Sailly Labourse	24/12/1915	27/12/1915
War Diary	Noyelles	28/12/1915	31/12/1915
Heading	1/23 London Regt Jan Vol XI		
War Diary	Section C.2	01/01/1916	05/01/1916
War Diary	Les Brebis	06/01/1916	08/01/1916
War Diary	Double Crassier	10/01/1916	18/01/1916
War Diary	Braquemont	18/01/1916	20/01/1916
War Diary	Loos	22/01/1916	28/01/1916
War Diary	Braquemont	29/01/1916	31/01/1916
Heading	23 London Regt Feb Vol XII		
War Diary	Braquemont	01/02/1916	20/02/1916
War Diary	Burbure	21/02/1916	07/03/1916
War Diary	Barlin	08/03/1916	09/03/1916
War Diary	Coupigny	10/03/1916	27/03/1916
Heading	1/23 London Regt Vol XIV April 1916		
War Diary	Lorette Heights	02/04/1916	20/04/1916
War Diary	Fresnicourt	21/04/1916	26/04/1916
War Diary	Bouvigny	27/04/1916	01/05/1916
War Diary	Souchez Sector	03/05/1916	08/05/1916
War Diary	Verdrel	09/05/1916	14/05/1916
War Diary	Villers	16/05/1916	26/05/1916
War Diary	Ourton	27/05/1916	31/05/1916
Heading	1/23 London Regt Vol XIII		
War Diary	Ourton	01/06/1916	13/06/1916
War Diary	Bouvigny Woods	14/06/1916	17/06/1916
War Diary	Angres I Section	21/06/1916	30/06/1916

Heading	142nd Brigade 47th Division 1/23rd Battalion London Regiment July 1916		
War Diary	Bouvigny Woods	01/07/1916	10/07/1916
War Diary	Bully Grenay	11/07/1916	23/07/1916
War Diary	Souchez Sector	24/07/1916	25/07/1916
War Diary	Villers Au Bois	26/07/1916	28/07/1916
War Diary	Ourton	29/07/1916	30/07/1916
War Diary	Averdoingt	31/07/1916	31/07/1916
Heading	142nd Brigade 47th Division 1/23rd Battalion London Regiment August 1916		
War Diary	Averdoingt	01/08/1916	01/08/1916
War Diary	Remaisnil	02/08/1916	03/08/1916
War Diary	Bernatre	04/08/1916	05/08/1916
War Diary	St. Riquier	06/08/1916	20/08/1916
War Diary	Francieres	21/08/1916	21/08/1916
War Diary	Vignacourt	22/08/1916	22/08/1916
War Diary	Villers Bocage	23/08/1916	23/08/1916
War Diary	Lahoussoye	24/08/1916	10/09/1916
War Diary	Albert	11/09/1916	22/09/1916
War Diary	Mellincourt	23/09/1916	31/10/1916
War Diary	Halifax Camp	01/11/1916	04/11/1916
War Diary	Belgian Chateau	05/11/1916	08/11/1916
War Diary	Dominion Lines	09/11/1916	30/11/1916
War Diary	Canal Sub Sector Ypres	01/12/1916	08/12/1916
War Diary	Dominion	09/12/1916	30/12/1916
War Diary	Hill 60 Sub Sector Ypres	01/01/1917	08/01/1917
War Diary	Dominion	09/01/1917	16/01/1917
War Diary	Dickebusch Huts	17/01/1917	27/01/1917
War Diary	Right Section Of Canal Sub Sector	28/01/1917	29/01/1917
War Diary	Bluff Sector	30/01/1917	01/02/1917
War Diary	Ypres	03/02/1917	04/02/1917
War Diary	Dominion	05/02/1917	17/02/1917
War Diary	Hill 60	17/02/1917	28/02/1917
War Diary	Dominion Camp	01/03/1917	07/03/1917
War Diary	Dickebusch	08/03/1917	14/03/1917
War Diary	Canal Sub Sector	19/03/1917	22/03/1917
War Diary	Dominion	23/03/1917	23/03/1917
War Diary	Steenvoorde	24/03/1917	24/03/1917
War Diary	Arneke	25/03/1917	25/03/1917
War Diary	Houlle	26/03/1917	31/03/1917
War Diary	Houlle P-De-C	01/04/1917	08/04/1917
War Diary	Arneke	09/04/1917	09/04/1917
War Diary	Steenvoorde	10/04/1917	11/04/1917
War Diary	Halifax	12/04/1917	19/04/1917
War Diary	Canal Sub Sector Ypres	22/04/1917	28/04/1917
War Diary	Ottawa	29/04/1917	06/05/1917
War Diary	Canal Sub Sector	07/05/1917	14/05/1917
War Diary	Ottawa	15/05/1917	21/05/1917
War Diary	Steenvoorde	22/05/1917	31/05/1917
War Diary	Canal Reserve Camp	01/06/1917	01/06/1917
War Diary	Devonshire	02/06/1917	05/06/1917
War Diary	Right Section Canal Sub Sector Ypres	07/06/1917	12/06/1917
War Diary	Kempton Park	13/06/1917	14/06/1917
War Diary	Caestre	15/06/1917	15/06/1917
War Diary	Racquinghem	17/06/1917	17/06/1917
War Diary	St Martin	18/06/1917	23/06/1917

War Diary	Racquinghem	24/06/1917	27/06/1917
War Diary	Meteren	28/06/1917	28/06/1917
War Diary	Ridge Wood	29/06/1917	29/06/1917
War Diary	Dammstrasse	30/06/1917	30/06/1917
Miscellaneous	Narrative Of 2nd Army Offensive Operation Of June 7th-9th 1917		
War Diary	Trenches Immediately S. Of Ypres Canal	01/07/1917	08/07/1917
War Diary	M.6.d.5.8	09/07/1917	15/07/1917
War Diary	Support	18/07/1917	28/07/1917
War Diary	Kempton Camp	29/07/1917	31/07/1917
War Diary	Kempton Park	01/08/1917	09/08/1917
War Diary	Zudausques	10/08/1917	17/08/1917
War Diary	Dominion	19/08/1917	20/08/1917
War Diary	Swan Chateau	21/08/1917	24/08/1917
War Diary	Westhoek	25/08/1917	02/09/1917
War Diary	Dominion	04/09/1917	05/09/1917
War Diary	Steenvoorde	06/09/1917	10/09/1917
War Diary	Dickebusch	11/09/1917	16/09/1917
War Diary	Vanoost	17/09/1917	18/09/1917
War Diary	Steenvoorde	19/09/1917	22/09/1917
War Diary	Wakefield Camp	23/09/1917	24/09/1917
War Diary	Oppy Front	25/09/1917	30/09/1917
War Diary	Railway Cutting	01/10/1917	10/10/1917
War Diary	St Aubin	11/10/1917	18/10/1917
War Diary	Gavrelle	21/10/1917	31/10/1917
War Diary	St Aubin	01/11/1917	03/11/1917
War Diary	Gavrelle	04/11/1917	05/11/1917
War Diary	Aubrey	06/11/1917	21/11/1917
War Diary	Le Pendu	22/11/1917	22/11/1917
War Diary	Birneville	23/11/1917	24/11/1917
War Diary	Gomiecourt	25/11/1917	25/11/1917
War Diary	Barastre	26/11/1917	27/11/1917
War Diary	Beaumetz	28/11/1917	28/11/1917
War Diary	Forward Area	29/11/1917	30/11/1917
Miscellaneous	Report On Raid Carried Out By 1/23rd Bn. The London Regt	06/11/1917	06/11/1917
War Diary	Forward Area 57.c N.E.	01/12/1917	08/12/1917
War Diary	57.C N.E	09/12/1917	15/12/1917
War Diary	Bertincourt	16/12/1917	17/12/1917
War Diary	Millencourt	18/12/1917	30/12/1917
War Diary	Etricourt	31/12/1917	31/12/1917
War Diary	Lechelle	01/01/1918	05/01/1918
War Diary	Ribecourt	07/01/1918	12/01/1918
War Diary	Bertincourt	14/01/1918	31/01/1918
War Diary	London Camp	02/02/1918	13/02/1918
War Diary	Ribecourt	13/02/1918	23/02/1918
War Diary	Rocquigny	24/02/1918	28/02/1918
Heading	47th Division 142nd Infantry Brigade 1/23rd Battalion London Regiment March 1918		
War Diary	Rocquigny	01/03/1918	23/03/1918
War Diary	Battle Zone	23/03/1918	31/03/1918
Heading	142nd Brigade 47th Division 1/23rd Battalion The London Regiment April 1918		
War Diary	Martinsart	01/04/1918	04/04/1918
War Diary	Aveluy Wood 57 D 1/20,000	05/04/1918	07/04/1918
War Diary	Warloy	08/04/1918	08/04/1918

War Diary	Raincheval	09/04/1918	10/04/1918
War Diary	Montrelet	11/04/1918	11/04/1918
War Diary	Yvrencheux	12/04/1918	30/04/1918
Miscellaneous	Report On The Operations At Aveluy Wood On 5th And 6th April 1918	05/04/1918	05/04/1918
War Diary	Warloy	01/05/1918	31/05/1918
War Diary	Bresle Lavieville	01/06/1918	01/06/1918
War Diary	Lahoussoye	05/06/1918	08/06/1918
War Diary	Left Sub Sector	09/06/1918	19/06/1918
War Diary	Left Subsector Albert	19/06/1918	19/06/1918
War Diary	Behencourt	20/06/1918	21/06/1918
War Diary	Bougainville	22/06/1918	12/07/1918
War Diary	Forward Area	12/07/1918	18/07/1918
War Diary	Warloy-Baillon	19/07/1918	21/07/1918
War Diary	Warloy	21/07/1918	21/07/1918
War Diary	Forward Area	21/07/1918	31/07/1918
Heading	142nd Bde 47th Div. 1/23rd Battalion London Regiment August 1918		
War Diary		01/08/1918	30/09/1918
War Diary	Buneville	01/10/1918	21/10/1918
War Diary	Busnes	22/10/1918	01/11/1918
War Diary	Willems	02/11/1918	10/11/1918
War Diary	Frasnes	11/11/1918	13/11/1918
War Diary	Kain	14/11/1918	15/11/1918
War Diary	Cysoing	16/11/1918	27/11/1918
War Diary	Burbure	28/11/1918	17/04/1919
War Diary	Floringhem	18/04/1919	03/05/1919

WO 95/2744 (1)
Mar '15 — Apr '19
1/23 London Regt

47TH DIVISION
142ND INFY BDE

1-23RD LONDON REGT.

MARCH 1915-APR 1919

47TH DIVISION
142ND INFY BDE

142nd Inf. Bde.

47th Division.

Batt<u>n</u>. disembarked Havre from England 15.3.15

[WAR DIARY]

1/23rd LONDON REGT.

MARCH

1915

(14.3.15 - 31.3.15)

Army Form C. 2118.

WAR DIARY
or
INTELLIGENCE SUMMARY

(Erase heading not required.)

Instructions regarding War Diaries and Intelligence Summaries are contained in F. S. Regs., Part II. and the Staff Manual respectively. Title pages will be prepared in manuscript.

Hour, Date, Place		Summary of Events and Information	Remarks and references to Appendices
14th March 1915.	St Albans.	Entrained two half Battalions for Southampton. Embarked 7pm s/s "Copenhagen", Transport on s/s "Trafford Hall"	
15th March 1915.	Havre	Disembarked 8 am. Marched to No 2 Rest Camp	
16th " 1915	Rest Camp	Marched 6.30 am. Entrained 10 am.	
17th " 1915	Argues.	Arrived 4 am. and billeted in close billets.	
18th " 1915	-do-	Company Training	
19th " 1915	-do-	Marched to Lesfesses. Billeted in close billets.	
20th " 1915	LESPESSES	Marched to St HILAIRE. -do-	
21st " 1915	ST HILAIRE	Divine Service.	
22nd " 1915	-do-	Company drill. Fire control, fire discipline &c	
23rd " 1915	-do-	" -do-	
24th " 1915	-do-	Digging, Physical training.	
25th " 1915	-do-	"filling in trenches. Company training.	
26th " 1915	-do-	Physical drill, bayonet fighting and Company training.	
27th " 1915	-do-	Marched to LABEUVRIERE.	
28th " 1915	LABEUVRIERE	Divine Service	
29th " 1915	-do-	Company training, Musketry (instructing snipers).	

Army Form C. 2118.

WAR DIARY
or
INTELLIGENCE SUMMARY
(Erase heading not required.)

Instructions regarding War Diaries and Intelligence Summaries are contained in F. S. Regs., Part II. and the Staff Manual respectively. Title pages will be prepared in manuscript.

Hour, Date, Place	Summary of Events and Information	Remarks and references to Appendices
30th March 1915. LABEUVRIERE	Physical Training, Coy. Training, digging by day and night.	
31st " 1915 –do–	–do– –do–	

Labeuvriere.
1/4/15.

Wm. E. Thornhill
Capt. a/adjt.
for Comdg. 23rd Battn. The London Regt.

142nd Inf. Bde.
47th Division.

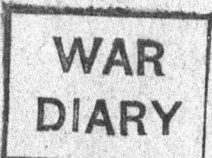

1/23rd LONDON REGT.

APRIL

1915

WAR DIARY or INTELLIGENCE SUMMARY

Army Form C. 2118.

(Erase heading not required.)

Instructions regarding War Diaries and Intelligence Summaries are contained in F. S. Regs., Part II. and the Staff Manual respectively. Title pages will be prepared in manuscript.

Hour, Date, Place	Summary of Events and Information	Remarks and references to Appendices
Lillers 1st April 1915	Company training. Trench digging. C & D Companies marched to mine No 3. BRUAY.	
2nd April 1915	Good Friday. Divine Service. An efficient lookout post established between 11 p.m and 7 a.m to watch for hostile Aircraft.	
3rd April 1915	Field training; fire control; trench digging.	
4th April 1915	Easter Sunday. Divine service. Lieut. V.O. Rees proceeded to Base, vice Capt. R.H. Auckland.	
5th April 1915	A & B. Coys. digging. "C" Coy. fire control. "D" Coy. digging in unit entrenching tools. Cooking in the field. Grenadier Coy. practice.	
6th April 1915.	A.B. & D. Coys. digging. "C" Coy. fire control & direction.	
7th April 1915.	Digging. All Companies bathed at N° 3 Mine, BRUAY.	
8th April 1915	Battalion marched to OBLINGHEM and billeted in close billets.	
9th April 1915. OBLINGHEM	Company drill. K.H. inspection &c.	
10th April 1915.	Bayonet fighting; Company drill. Capt. R.H. Auckland joined from Base vice Lt. V.O. Rees.	
11th April 1915.	Batt. marched to EES GLAUQMES. Companies entered the trenches as follows:—	

Army Form C. 2118.

WAR DIARY
or
INTELLIGENCE SUMMARY.
(Erase heading not required.)

Instructions regarding War Diaries and Intelligence Summaries are contained in F.S. Regs., Part II. and the Staff Manual respectively. Title pages will be prepared in manuscript.

Place	Date	Hour	Summary of Events and Information	Remarks and references to Appendices
LES GLAUGNES	11/4/15		"A" Coy went 1st Coldstream Guards — for instruction	
"	12/4/15		"B" " 1st Black Watch — for instruction	
"	13/4/15		"C" " 1st Cameron Highlanders	
"	14/4/15		"D" " London Scottish	
"	14/4/15		Casualties 2 wounded (one died of wounds 14/4/15)	
"	15/4/15		1 Killed (Pte G.F. Barden)	
"	16/4/15		3 wounded (including 1 Officer). Burial of Pte G Barden at RICHEBOURG St VAAST "B" at Arras in Town Cemetery, BETHUNE	
"	17/4/15		1 wounded	
"	18/4/15		3 wounded	
"	19/4/15		1 Killed (Pte W DRURY) 2 wounded	
"	19/4/15		2 wounded. Burial of Pte Drury at RICHEBOURG St VAAST.	
		3 pm	The Batt. Headqrs were moved to MESPLAUX. The Batt. left the trenches about 8.30 pm + killed at MESPLAUX and LES FACONS	
MESPLAUX	20/4/15	10.15 am	Batt. marched out of MESPLAUX and marched to ALLOUAGNE, arriving at 2.30 pm + killed	
ALLOUAGNE	21/4/15		Inspections of Kit, rifles, ammunition, iron rations &c	
	22/4/15		Batt. marched to AUCHEL by Companies for bathing	

WAR DIARY
or
INTELLIGENCE SUMMARY.
(Erase heading not required.)

Army Form C. 2118.

Place	Date	Hour	Summary of Events and Information	Remarks and references to Appendices
ALLOUAGNE	23/4/15		Battn. marched to LONG CORNET & billets there and at LES CHOQUAUX (Headquarters).	
LES CHOQUAUX	24/4/15	4.30 p.m.	Transport moved to ESSARS. 2/Lt R.M. Ballard & 43 N.C.O.s & men joined from Base.	
		6.30 p.m.	The Battn. (less Transport) marched to trenches (section D.1). Headqrs. at RUE DU BOIS.	
RUE DU BOIS	25/4/15		Casualties 2 wounded. "C" Company in local reserve	
	26/4/15		" 1 " "	
	27/4/15		" 1 " men wounded 26/4/15 (4/Cpl. R. Vernon) died of wounds & buried in town cemetery, BETHUNE	
	28/4/15		" 2 " (One, 4/Sgt. J.G. Allen, died of wounds).	
	29/4/15		4/Sgt. J.G. Allen buried in town cemetery, BETHUNE.	
	28/4/15	8.15 p.m.	Battn. relieved from trenches by 2nd Battn. Headqrs. & left half Battn. billeted at LE TOURET.	
			Right half under Major H.S.J. Stansfeld at RUE DE L'EPINETTE.	
LE TOURET	29/4/15		Working parties of 4 Officers, 200 men (half at 8.30 p.m., second half 11.30 p.m.)	
			During day, inspection of kits, &c. First aid class under M.O. at 2.30 p.m.	
	30/4/15		Company drills, inspections as on 29/4/15. First aid class at 2.30 p.m.	
	"	11 p.m.	Working party of 2 Officers & 100 men at INDIAN VILLAGE.	
			Casualties – 1 wounded.	

Wm. E. Thornhill Capt M
for Cmdr 23 Lon Regt

1577 Wt.W10791/1773 500,000 1/15 D.D. & L. A.D.S.S./Forms/C. 2118.

142nd Inf. Bde.
47th Division.

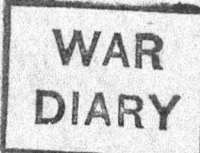

1/23rd LONDON REGT.

MAY

1915

Attached.
Appendix I.

Army Form C. 2118.

WAR DIARY
or
INTELLIGENCE SUMMARY

(Erase heading not required.)

Instructions regarding War Diaries and Intelligence Summaries are contained in F. S. Regs., Part II. and the Staff Manual respectively. Title pages will be prepared in manuscript.

Hour, Date, Place	Summary of Events and Information	Remarks and references to Appendices
LE TOURET P.M. 1st May 1915. 11.30	Provided working party of 1 Officer + 50 men at communication trench from BOMB HOUSE to BUTT "3.E."	
2nd May 1915 11 a.m.	Working Party of 1 Officer + 50 men to carry hurdles to D1 - (c) 50 " " " ORCHARD communication trench.	
9 p.m.	Church Parade. Inspection of kilts by Commanding Officer. Working party of 2 Officers 100 men at ORCHARD communication trench (2 parties of 1 Off. + 50 men each).	
3rd May 1915 4.15	Working party of 2 NCOs + 20 men at CHOCOLAT MENIER CORNER. " " " 2 Officers + 80 " " communication trench from BOMB HOUSE to BUTT "E". Capt. A.J. Clark admitted Hospital. Battn. left LE TOURET + RUE DE L'EPINETTE + entered trenches, relieving 2d Bn London Regt. (D'Company in Local Reserve), in Section D1 (C + D). Capt. R.H. Auchhild attached to command 'A' Coy in absence of Capt. A. J. Clark (Hospital)	
RUE DU BOIS 4th May 1915	Casualties - 1 wounded (Pte R.A. Mills). Working party repairing breastworks + wire in front of trenches. Corpl. Phillips a 2 men of "A" Coy rejoined from course of instruction in trench mortar battery.	

Army Form C. 2118.

WAR DIARY
or
INTELLIGENCE SUMMARY
(Erase heading not required.)

Instructions regarding War Diaries and Intelligence Summaries are contained in F. S. Regs., Part II. and the Staff Manual respectively. Title pages will be prepared in manuscript.

Hour, Date, Place	Summary of Events and Information	Remarks and references to Appendices
RUE DU BOIS 5/5/1915.	Sgt. S. Perrons + 3 men sent to LABEUVRIERE for some in shooting with telescopic sights.	
6/5/1915	Casualties. 8 wounded. 1 Killed (Pte Rayner JA) Bruise of Rifle. Rayner at cemetery near LE TOURET. Battn. relieved from trenches by 24th Battn. London Regt., commencing at 8.15 p.m. Battn. marched by Companies to LE PREOL. Transport at BEUVRY. Capt. Brindel admitted to Hospital.	
LE PREOL 7/5/1915	Interior economy. 9 Control posts (1 NCO + 3 men each) taken over.	
8/5/1915	Parades by Companies for inspections of Rifles, ammn. &c. 9 a.m. "A" Coy under Sgt. Major 10.30 a.m. "B" " " " 11.30 a.m. Bathing in afternoon. All blankets handed in to R.Q.M Stores.	
9/5/1915 3.30 a.m.	Battn. stood to arms + occupied reserve trenches in neighbourhood of LEPREOL. Breakfast in trenches at 6 a.m. Battalion returned to Billets commencing at 8.30 a.m. (by Platoons).	
10/5/1915 5 a.m 11 a.m. 9 p.m.	Battn. stood to arms on Coy parade grounds till 5.15 a.m. Interior economy and bathing in cadre. Inspection of Rifles by C.O. Battn. paraded and marched to Major Gt. London Infantry Bde.	

WAR DIARY
or
INTELLIGENCE SUMMARY

Army Form C. 2118.

Hour, Date, Place	Summary of Events and Information	Remarks and references to Appendices
LE PREOL 11/5/15	Entire morning bathing.	
12/5/15	Batt. paraded at 1.45 p.m. and marched to OBLINGHEM and billeted in billets occupied on April 8th 1915.	
13/5/15	Interior economy, rifle + kit inspections.	
14/5/15	Batt. part 3 a.m. and marched to trenches at CUINCHY (Section A 1) on the extreme right of the British line, relieving 2nd Bn Worcester Reg't. C & D Coy fire trenches, A in support, B Battalion Reserve. HdQrs in dugouts on Bedford Row.	
CUINCHY 17/5/15	Relieved at 8 a.m. by 2nd Battn. The London Reg't, billeted at TOURBIERES, except one note from Beaufort Rois, "C" Company remained in trenches.	
TOURBIERES 18/5/15	Pte M. Bates, No. 1095 (attached Trench Mortar Battery) wounded	
" 19/5/15	Working party of 2 Officers & 150 men provided for work in widening road. Lead by 2/Lt S.V. Shenington proceeded to England.	
20/5/15	Corpl. Rogers + Pte J. Carry (D Coy) joined 170th Mining Coy. R.E. Re-entered trenches at 8 p.m. in relation A 1, relieving 24th Bn London Reg't. No. 3101, Pte ? H Elliott Killed.	
CUINCHY 21/5/15	Burial of Pte Elliott in 1st R. Berks Reg't cemetery behind Section A 1. Batt. relieved at 2 p.m. by 2nd Gloucester Reg't and marched to BEUVRY billeting in close billets. Two men killed by Germans during late afternoon and evening resulting in death of No 2769 Corpl S Edwards, No. 2510 Pte J. Leonard, No. 2185 Pte. C. Dawe + Pte H Waters, & wounded of No. 2218 Pte R.W. Read.	

Army Form C. 2118.

WAR DIARY
or
INTELLIGENCE SUMMARY

(Erase heading not required.)

Instructions regarding War Diaries and Intelligence Summaries are contained in F.S. Regs., Part II. and the Staff Manual respectively. Title pages will be prepared in manuscript.

Hour, Date, Place		Summary of Events and Information	Remarks and references to Appendices
BEUVRY	22/5/15	Burial of Pte H Watney in Local Churchyard. Capt V.S.D. Wallis, Capt R.H. Archbold + Lieut R.A. Berry attached to hospital suffering from concussion through explosion of shell. Officers did reconnaissance in trenches at GIVENCHY.	
—	23/5/15	Divine service under Company arrangements.	
—	24/5/15	Battalion left at 2 p.m. by Companies + relieved 22nd Bn London Regt in trenches at GIVENCHY. "C" Company fire trenches "D" Coy in support & "B" Coy in reserve. Bn HdQrs at WINDY CORNER.	
GIVENCHY	25/5/15	Orders received in afternoon that Batt. was to attack German trench at J.7, 1000 yards S. Casualties 4 officers + 99, including 3 Officers killed + 10 wounded.	See Appendix I
—	26/5/15	Batt. relieved from captured German trench by 20th Bn. The London Regt + commanded to leave trenches at 3 p.m. Marched to LE QUESNOL - HELUTA. Lieut 7. Saturnode appointed to command No 1 Coy (A & B Coys amalgamated)	
LE QUESNOL	27/5/15	Draft of 122 men received from Damon no being buried	
—	28/5/15	Batt. addressed by Br. Lt. C.C. Munro, accompanied by Major-Gen Bartho, G.O.C. 47th (London) Division.	
—	29/5/15	Interior economy & refitting.	
—	30/5/15	Refitting. Divine Service Companies at 10 a.m.	

Army Form C. 2118.

WAR DIARY
or
INTELLIGENCE SUMMARY

(Erase heading not required.)

Instructions regarding War Diaries and Intelligence Summaries are contained in F. S. Regs., Part II. and the Staff Manual respectively. Title pages will be prepared in manuscript.

Hour, Date, Place	Summary of Events and Information	Remarks and references to Appendices
LE QUESNOL 30/5/15	Church Parade at 3 p.m., conducted by Brigade Chaplain. Service attended by Brig. Genl. Cuntry, 142nd Infantry Bde. and Staff.	
— 31/5/15	Battalion bathed at BETHUNE by Companies. Capt. Saffery & Lieut. Priddeley (21st Bn. London Regt) attached for duty.	

5/6/15

Wm. E. Thornhill.
Capt. & Adjt.
for Comdg. 23rd Battn. The London Regiment

APPENDIX I

Appendix I.

Report on Operations May 25-26th 1915.   (COPY).

To Brig. Genl. Commanding   28/5/15
    142nd Infantry Bde.
From O.C. 23rd Bn. The London Regt.

Sir,
    I have the honour to report as follows on the operations on the 25-26th inst. in which this Battalion took part & to bring the undermentioned names of Officers, N.C.Os & men to your notice for your consideration:-

    The assault was ordered for 6.30 p.m. and at this hour No. 13 & 14 platoons of "D" Coy., [led by Lieut. Wood and C.S.M. Hammond] went over the parapet as one man and captured their allotted section of the enemy trench at the cost of about 14 casualties.

    There was very great congestion in our communication trenches at this time & there was some difficulty in feeding the supporting platoons into Scottish Trench. This was remedied by advancing the supports across the open from NEW CUT to SCOTTISH TRENCH.

    Two telephone wires were sent out with the leading platoons, & I was in communication with the captured trench three minutes after it had been taken.

    The battalion advanced by double platoons at regular intervals & by about 8 p.m. the whole battalion was in the captured trench.

    At about 8.45 p.m. I received a message that the captured trench was being badly enfiladed by rifle & machine gun fire from the left. Our machine guns went into action from UPPER CUT but were unable to prevent this fire continuing.

    The telephone then broke down & though several efforts were made to run out another line, the wire was always cut.

    During the whole night very heavy casualties were suffered by the Battalion as they were being enfiladed from both sides. In fact the shrapnel & H.E. fire from the right was enfilading our section of the trench at an angle of about 6° from the rear.

142nd Inf. Bde.
47th Division.

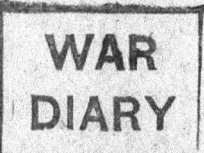

1/23rd LONDON REGT.

JUNE

1915

WAR DIARY or INTELLIGENCE SUMMARY

Army Form C. 2118.

(Erase heading not required.)

Instructions regarding War Diaries and Intelligence Summaries are contained in F.S. Regs., Part II. and the Staff Manual respectively. Title pages will be prepared in manuscript.

Hour, Date, Place		Summary of Events and Information	Remarks and references to Appendices
LE QUESNOY			
1st June 1915	9 p.m.	Battn. paraded and marched to VERQUIN. 2/Lt A.P. Clarke returned to duty from Machine Gun Course	
2nd "		Company parades for kit, rifle & inspections.	
3rd "	6.30 a.m.	Physical training. } Battn. organized into 2 Companies — No 1 = A + B	
	9 a.m.	Battn. inspected by C.O. } — 2 = C + D	
		2/Lt A.P. Clarke appointed Machine Gun Officer. (Temporarily.)	
4th "	9 a.m.	Route march	
		Sergt. Cockram + 3 men detailed as Sharpshooters.	
5th "	9 a.m.	Route march	
6th "	11.30 "	Church parade.	
	9 p.m.	Battn. paraded and marched to LES BREBIS, arriving at midnight. No 1 Coy in reserve at LES BREBIS, No 2 Coy in house reserve at MAROC. temporarily attached to 24th Battn. The London Regt.	
7th "		Bathing parades	
8th "	8 p.m.	Working party of 1 Officer + 100 men for work with 22nd Battn.	
9th "	2 a.m.	" returned from W. 2. Trenches.	
	8 a.m.	" of 1 Officer + 50 men for work in trenches.	
10th "	11.30 p.	Battn. relieved 24th Battn. in section W, one Coy of 24th Bn L.R. in local reserve at MAROC.	
	2.30 p.m.	Voluntary service at LES BREBIS conducted by Brigade Chaplain	
11th		Our trenches subjected to terrific fire by enemy, but no casualties sustained.	

Army Form C. 2118.

WAR DIARY
or
INTELLIGENCE SUMMARY
(Erase heading not required.)

Instructions regarding War Diaries and Intelligence Summaries are contained in F. S. Regs., Part II. and the Staff Manual respectively. Title pages will be prepared in manuscript.

Hour, Date, Place			Summary of Events and Information	Remarks and references to Appendices
MAROC				
15th June 1915	4 p.m.		Continued artillery and rifle fire opened on German trenches, covering advance of 4th Corps on north and French troops on south.	
			Casualties 1 Killed (4/gr. A.P. Bird) and 9 wounded.	
16th	"		4/gr. A. P. Bird buried in churchyard of ruined church near MAROC, by Brigade Chaplain.	
			Casualties – 3 wounded. Capt. A.T. Farrantines K.duty from England.	
17th	"	11 p.m.	Battn. relieved by 24th Battn. and marched to old billets at LES BREBIS.	
	LES BREBIS		No 1 Coy remaining at MAROC in local reserve.	
18th	"	9 a.m.	Bathing and refitting	
19th	"	"	" inspection parades	
		8 p.m.	Working party of 1 Officer & 30 men to carry wire for R.E.	
20th	"	10 a.m.	Church parade.	
			Battn. relieved by 19th Battn. London Regt. and marched to rest billets at NOEUX-LES-MINES.	
21st June	NOEUX-les-MINES		Rifle + Kit inspections.	
22nd	"	9 a.m.	Company drill	
		6 p.m.	Physical training	
			1st Col. Bradfield proceeded to England on leave.	
23rd	"	6.30 a.m.	Physical Training	
			No 1 Coy. under Sergt Major at 10.30 a.m. for drill	
		2 "	by arrangements	
			Lieut. L.S. Cluton reported for duty from England.	

Army Form C. 2118.

WAR DIARY
or
INTELLIGENCE SUMMARY

(Erase heading not required.)

Instructions regarding War Diaries and Intelligence Summaries are contained in F.S. Regs., Part II. and the Staff Manual respectively. Title pages will be prepared in manuscript.

Hour, Date, Place	Summary of Events and Information	Remarks and references to Appendices
NOEUX-les-MINES		
24th June 1915. 9 a.m.	Route march (1 platoon of each company) under Capt. Fearon Armstrong.	
" 11 "	Training of all men as bombers and bayonet men.	
25th " 6.30 a.m.	Physical training.	
" 9 a.m.	Route march — 1 platoon. Remainder of Battn. training as Grenadiers and bayonet men.	
26th " 6.30 a.m.	Physical training.	
" 9.30 "	Training bombers and bayonet to work in conjunction.	
" 11 a.m.	No. 2 Coy. inspected by Medical Officer.	
27th " 8.30 a.m.	Church parade (Nonconformists)	
" 10.45 "	" " (Roman Catholics)	
" 11 a.m.	" "	
" 11.30 "	Inspection of No. 1 Coy. in marching order	
" 11.50 "	" " " 2 " " "	
28th " "	Inspection of billets, rifles, ammunition &c.	
" 8.30 p.m.	Battn. paraded and marched to Section X2, relieving 7th Bn. London Regt.	
"Section X2" 11 p.m.	Lt. Col. H. Streatfield returned from leave.	
29th " "	Lieut. F. Entwistle proceeded to England on 7 days' leave, via Bethune.	

JMc E Thornhill
for Comdg. 23rd Bn. The London Regt.
Capt. + Adjt.

142nd Inf. Bde.
47th Division.

WAR DIARY

1/23rd LONDON REGT.

JULY

1915

Army Form C. 2118.

WAR DIARY
or
INTELLIGENCE SUMMARY
(Erase heading not required.)

Instructions regarding War Diaries and Intelligence Summaries are contained in F. S. Regs., Part II. and the Staff Manual respectively. Title pages will be prepared in manuscript.

Hour, Date, Place	Summary of Events and Information	Remarks and references to Appendices
SECTION X2.		
1st July 1915	Covering party of 1 N.C.O. & 6 men for wiring parties.	
2nd "	No 1 Coy. relieved by Coy. of 24th & held in reserve in QUALITY ST.	
" 9-12 a.m.	1 N.C.O. & 12 men for instruction in wiring	
6th " 5 p.m.	No 1 Coy. relieved No 2 Coy. which returned to QUALITY ST. in reserve.	
7th "	Lieut. Entwistle returned from leave.	
" 10 p.m.	1 N.C.O. & 6 men as covering party for wirers at SAP 13.	
8th " 10 p.m.	1 " " 6 " " " " " " SAP 12a.	
9th " p.m.	Work on Trench 9a to 12 & communication Trench 9f.	
" 10 p.m.	1 N.C.O. & 6 men as covering party for wirers at SAP 9a.	
"	Lieut Macmillan, R.A.M.C. (attd) proceeded on leave.	
10th " 10 p.m.	1 N.C.O. & 6 men as covering party to wirers at SAP 12.	
" p.m.	Completion of work on Trench 12 to 9a. Line A, & improvement of trenches 12 & 9f. from line B to line A.	
" p.m.	Work on shelters in Lines A & B & in keeps commenced.	
" 8 p.m.	No 2 Coy moved up to shelters in second line in X2, together with companies of 21st & 24th Bns. 2 Coys. 22nd Bn. billeted in Quality St. in local reserve.	
11th " 10 p.m.	1 N.C.O. & 6 men as covering party to wirers at SAP 12.	

Army Form C. 2118.

WAR DIARY
or
INTELLIGENCE SUMMARY
(Erase heading not required.)

Instructions regarding War Diaries and Intelligence Summaries are contained in F.S. Regs., Part II. and the Staff Manual respectively. Title pages will be prepared in manuscript.

Hour, Date, Place	Summary of Events and Information	Remarks and references to Appendices
SECTION X 2		
14th July 1915. PM MAZINGARBE	Battn. relieved by 17th Bn London Regt. and marched by Platoons to MAZINGARBE in Divisional Reserve.	
15" 8.30	Inspections of rifles &c., interior economy (Coy.)	
16"	Capt. J.E. Thorneycroft proceeded on leave.	
17" 7.30 pm	Working party of 3 Officers & 100 men provided. (No 1 Coy) Lieut. L.S. Clinton proceeded to M.G. course at WISQUES. 2/Lt. A.P. Clarke after M.G.O. in absence of Lt Clinton. 2 Officers 21st Bn attached for duty. Lt Macmillan returned from leave.	
7.30 pm	Working party of 3 Officers + 100 men. (No 2 Coy)	
18" 7.30 "	" " " 3 " 100 "	
19" 7.30 "	" " " 3 " 100 "	
20 7.30 "	" " " 3 " 100 "	
21 7.30 "	" " " 3 " 100 "	
22nd 9 p.m.	2/Lt A.P. Clarke wounded. 2/Lt Phillips (Trench Mortar Battery) accidentally wounded. Battn. relieved 6th Bn London Regt. in section W.3. No 1 Coy in reserve billets at MAROC (& Headquarters) " 2 " " support trenches, work 1 Platoon in KEEP "D".	
23rd 9.30 p.m.	Covering party of 1 N.C.O & 12 men for wiring at Communication Trench No 24.	

WAR DIARY or INTELLIGENCE SUMMARY

Army Form C. 2118.

SECTION W.3.

Hour, Date, Place	Summary of Events and Information	Remarks and references to Appendices
24th July 1915. 7pm	Battn. relieved 24th Bn. in front line. 1 Coy (B) 1/4 "B" H.L.I. attached for instruction (No 5 + 6 Platoons attached to No 1 Coy); 7 + 8 to No 2 Coy). 2/Lt A.P. Clarke died of wounds at No 1 Dressing Shop; CHOCQUES. Working party on lines A + B + Keeps.	
25th July 1915	— do — — do — — do —	
26th " 1915 7pm	Battn. relieved by 24th Bn. in trenches. A + 1 Coy in support. No 2 Coy in reserve billets MAROC. 1 Coy 12th Bn A.I.S. attached for instruction. Work — KEEP "D".	
27th " 1915	" " " "D"	
28th " 1915	Battn. relieved 24th Bn. in front line (No 2 Coy on Right, No 1 Coy on left). 1 Coy 9th D. Black Watch attached for instruction. Work on lines A + B + KEEP D.	
30th " 1915 7pm	Battn. relieved in front line by 24th Bn. No 2 in support, No 1 Coy in reserve billets at MAROC. Work on Keeps and lines A + B.	
31st " 1915	Work on Keeps and lines A + B.	

JH E Thornhill Capt & Adjt
For Cmdg, 23rd Battn. The London Regt.

142nd Inf. Bde.
47th Division.

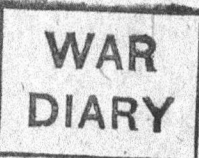

1/23rd LONDON REGT.

AUGUST

1915

Army Form C. 2118.

WAR DIARY
or
INTELLIGENCE SUMMARY
(Erase heading not required.)

Instructions regarding War Diaries and Intelligence Summaries are contained in F.S. Regs., Part II. and the Staff Manual respectively. Title pages will be prepared in manuscript.

Hour, Date, Place		Summary of Events and Information	Remarks and references to Appendices
SECTION W.3.			
1st August 1915		Work on Keeps.	
2nd " 1915		Capt. H Rathwell returned from leave.	
		Batt" relieved in Section W.3 by 9th Br Black Watch and marched to bivouac near HOUCHAIN.	
HOUCHAIN			
3rd August 1915	8 am	Batt" marched to LOZINGHEM, arriving 12.15 p.m.	
	2 p.m.	Lt. S. Christie returned from M.G. School.	
		Lt 7 Sturrock & 4 N.C.Os went to Bombing Course.	
LOZINGHEM			
4th August 1915	a.m.	Interior economy.	
	2 pm	No 1 Coy. bathed at AUCHEL	
	3.15 pm	" 2 " " "	
5th " 1915		Route march.	
6th " 1915		Physical training. Refitting and inspection.	
7th " 1915	9 a.m.	6 miles route march. 2/Lt G.A Ballard app\td Batt" Grenadier officer. 2/Lt G.C Turner to M.G School. Lt Sturrock returned from Bombing Course. [(?) Capt Whitely to England. 2nd in Comd Reserve]	
8th " 1915	9.30 am	Divine Service.	
9th " 1915	6.30 am	1 hr Physical training	
	9 "	1 " Company Drill	
	10.30 "	Route march (6 miles). Inspection of marching order.	
10th " 1915	7 am	No 1 Coy bathed at AUCHEL	
	6.30 am	" 2 " Physical training (1hr)	
	9 am	" 2 " Company drill (1hr.)	
	10.30	Batt" Route march (6 miles).	

WAR DIARY
or
INTELLIGENCE SUMMARY

(Erase heading not required.)

Army Form C. 2118.

Instructions regarding War Diaries and Intelligence Summaries are contained in F. S. Regs., Part II. and the Staff Manual respectively. Title pages will be prepared in manuscript.

Hour, Date, Place	Summary of Events and Information	Remarks and references to Appendices
LOZINGHEM P.M.		
10th August 1915. 3.30	No 2 Coy. bathed at AUCHEL.	
11th " 9.15 a.m.	Battn. paraded and marched to NOEUX-les-MINES.	
	Transport at HOUCHAIN. M.G. Section with 22nd Bn L.R.	
NOEUX-les-MINES.		
12th August 1915. 6.30 "	No 2 Coy. working party for digging 3rd line trenches at	
13th " 11. am	"	
" 6.30 a.m	"	
" 11. "	Capt. at Frames proceeded on leave to England. 2/Lt Cannon 21st Bn (attd.) R.Rine	
14th " 6.30 "	No 2 Coy. working party for digging 3rd line trenches at	
" 11. am	"	
15th " 6.30 "	"	
" 11. "	— do —	
16th " 6.30 "	— do —	2/Lt G.A. Bullard attended
" 11. "	— do —	Lewis Gun School, also 10 men
17th " 6.30 "	— do —	
" 11. "	— do —	
18th " 6.30 "	— do — accompanied by cooker	
" 9. "	8 men sent to army course at Noeux-les-Mines	
" 9.15 "	Battn. paraded and marched to ALLOUAGNE, picking up	
	Transports at HOUCHAIN, arriving 1.10 p.m.	

WAR DIARY
or
INTELLIGENCE SUMMARY

(Erase heading not required.)

Army Form C. 2118.

Hour, Date, Place	Summary of Events and Information	Remarks and references to Appendices
ALLOUAGNE.		
19th August 1915. 4 p.m.	Interior economy & refitting. Battalion inspected by Commanding Officer. Marching Order.	
20th " 1915 6.30 am	Physical training	
9.15 am	Companies paraded & marched to range for musketry. Lieut L.S. Clinton proceeded on leave.	
21st " 1915 6.30 am	Physical training. 125 N.C.O. & men joined from Base.	
10 a.m.	Inspection by Brig. Genl. 2/Lt G.Q. BALIAR	
22nd " 1915 9 am	Divine Service conducted by Brigade Chaplain. Capt. Q.J. HEARON returned from leave.	
10.30 "	Draft inspected by C.O.	
23rd " 1915 6.30 a	Physical training	
9 a.m.	Coy. training. Draft drilled by Seign. Major.	
10.45 "	Route march. 11 Officers joined from Base.	
24th " 1915 6.30	Physical training	
9 am	Coy. training.	
10.45 "	Route march. 2/Lt G.C. TURNER returned from Machine Gun School.	

Army Form C. 2118.

WAR DIARY
or
INTELLIGENCE SUMMARY
(Erase heading not required.)

Instructions regarding War Diaries and Intelligence Summaries are contained in F. S. Regs., Part II. and the Staff Manual respectively. Title pages will be prepared in manuscript.

Hour, Date, Place		Summary of Events and Information	Remarks and references to Appendices
ALLOUAGNE			
25th August 1915.	6.30 a.m.	Physical training.	
	p.m.	47th (London) Div. Sports.	
26" " 1915	6.30 a.m.	Physical training.	
	9 a.m.	Coy training.	
	10.15 - 1 p.m.	Squad + Coy. drill. Extended order drill &c &c	
	5 p.m.	Class of instruction for Subalterns + N.C.O.s.	
27" " 1915	6.30 a.m.	Physical training.	
	9 a.m. - 2 p.m.	Musketry.	
28" " 1915	6.30 a.m.	Physical training.	
	9 "	Coy training. Elementary musketry, &c &c	
29" " 1915.	6.30 "	Physical training	
	9 "	Coy "	
	10 "	Inspection of Lewis by C.O.	
	11.25 "	Divine Service	
30" " 1915	6.30 "	Physical training. Route march.	
	9 "	Coy Training. Route march.	
	3 p.m.	Bathing Parade.	
31st " 1915	6.15 a.m.	Batt. paraded + marched to HOUCHAIN. Motor buses conveyed Battn. to UPPENHILL. On arrival Battn. found working party on communication trenches. LES BRÉBIS.	

V/M E Uppenhill
Capt. & Adjt.
23rd Bn. The London Regt.

142nd Bde.
47th Division.

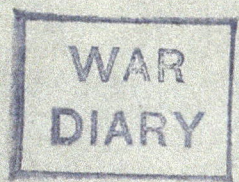

1/23rd LONDON REGIMENT

S&E&PTEMBER

1 9 1 5

INTELLIGENCE SUMMARY

(Erase heading not required.)

Instructions regarding War [Diaries and Intelligence] Summaries are contained in F.S. Regs., Part II. and the Staff Manual respectively. Title pages will be prepared in manuscript.

Hour, Date, Place	Summary of Events and Information	Remarks and references to Appendices
LES BREBIS		
1st Septr. 1915. 6.45 p.m.	Battn. (less 1 platoon) found working party for work on new front line trench in W.3	
2nd " 1915	Battn. formed working party on communication trenches behind W.3. Battn. billeted in S.MAROC in reserve.	
3rd " 1915 SECTOR W.3	Battn. relieved 6th Bn. Lon. Regt. in W.3.	
4th " 1915	2 men killed, 2 wounded.	
5th " 1915	Battn. still in W.3. Nothing of special note.	
10th " 1915		
11th Septr. 1915	Draft of 114 men arrived from the Base.	
12th " "	Nothing of special note.	
13 " "		
14 " "		
15th " 1915	Capt. O.R. Bare & Lt. R.S. Savoury (22nd Bn. Lon. Regt) attached for duty.	
16th " 1915	Battn. re-organised into 4 Companies. Major T.G.W. NEWMAN, 17th Bn. Lon. Regt, assumed command of Battn.	
17th " 1915	"A" Coy. in reserve in N.MAROC.	
19th " 1915	B " " " " " relieving A Coy	
21st " 1915	D " " " " " B "	

Hour, Date, Place	Summary of Events and Information	Remarks and references to Appendices
SECTOR W.3. 8 p.m. 23rd Septr. 1915.	Battn. relieved in W.3 by 17th Bn. Lon. Regt. & marched by platoons to LES BREBIS.	
LES BREBIS. 24th Septr. 1915 2 p.m.	150 men of A, C & D Coys. found working party in W.3. Overcoats & small kits packed in School by Coys. Capt. J. E. THORNHILL (Adjt.) (2nd Bn.Alpha) appointed to command 4th Bn. Royal Welch Fus. (T.F.) Capt. G.A. BRETT appointed Acting Adjt.	
25th 1915 2 a.m.	Battn. paraded & took up position in trenches (reserve) at FOSSE No 6, LES BREBIS.	
10.30 a.m.	Orders received for Battn. to proceed to W.3. & relieve 17th Bn. Lon. Regt. 2 Coys. in captured German trenches, 2 in W.3 (original front line). Battn. attached to 141st Inf Bde Casualties; 4 wounded.	
26th 1915	Whole Battn. moved to German second line trench outside LOOS. Headqrs. near CEMETERY.	
27th 1915 9 a.m.	"D" Coy. & Regimental Grenadier Platoon attached to 20th B'n: attacked & captured spoil near CHALK PIT, S. of LOOS & entrenched themselves on other side. 2/Lt G.A. BALLARD missing. Lcy. Sergt. Major. Thos. HAMMOND killed (First W.O. to lose his life in the Batn.) 1 Killed & 28 wounded in addition. (also 6 men gassed) Germans shelled our trenches with gas shells. Casualties: 2/Lt. R.C. BARKWORTH wounded.	

Hour, Date, Place	Summary of Events and Information	Remarks and references to Appendices
LOOS. 28th Septr. 1915	Day occupied in consolidating position. At night 141st Inf. Bde. was relieved by 142nd Inf. Bde., Battn. returning to duty unit latter. "B" & "C" Coy remained in German second line, while "A" & "D" Coys. moved back to German first line. I am relieved.	
29th 1915	Battn. relieved 22nd Bn. in German second line south of CEMETERY. "B" Coy. attached to 22nd Bn. & moved to advanced line on HILL 70. Casualties 3 men wounded.	
30th 1915.	Consolidation of position. 4 killed, 15 wounded.	
5th October 1915.		

G.L.B.D.S. Capt. & a/Adjt.
for Comdg. 23rd Battn. The London Regt.

142nd Inf. Bde.
47th Division.

WAR DIARY

1/23rd LONDON REGT.

OCTOBER

1915

Army Form C. 2118.

WAR DIARY
or
INTELLIGENCE SUMMARY

(Erase heading not required.)

Instructions regarding War Diaries and Intelligence Summaries are contained in F. S. Regs., Part II. and the Staff Manual respectively. Title pages will be prepared in manuscript.

Hour, Date, Place		Summary of Events and Information	Remarks and references to Appendices
LOOS			
1st October 1915	6 pm	Battn. relieved by French Colonial Troops and marched to Bivouac near LES BREBIS.	
LES BREBIS.			
2nd October 1915	8.30 am	Battn. paraded and marched to FOUQUIERES and billeted.	
FOUQUIERES			
3rd October 1915	11 am	Voluntary Church service	
	3 pm	Inspection by C.O.	
4th 1915	11 am	Route march	
		Grenadier platoon paraded for reconstruction.	
5th 1915	10 am	Coy and close order drill	
	12.30 pm	Bayonet fighting	
		Capt H Kethen Wiseman on leave to England.	
6th 1915		Battn marched to NOEUX-les-MINES.	
NOEUX-les-MINES.			
7th Octr 1915	9 am	"A"&"B" Coys. paraded and marched to area (K 16 B) ref 36 B sheet
	9.15	" " " " " (K 11 B) -do-
		"C"&"D" " " " " " "	
		and carried out 1 hr Close Order Drill & 1 hr Bayonet Exercises.	
8th	9 am	-do-	
	9.15	"	
	3.15 pm	Riding School for subaltern officers.	
		Capt. A.H. Kemble, 15th Bn. of our Regt reported for duty as Second in Command.	

WAR DIARY
or
INTELLIGENCE SUMMARY

(Erase heading not required.)

Army Form C. 2118.

Instructions regarding War Diaries and Intelligence Summaries are contained in F. S. Regs., Part II. and the Staff Manual respectively. Title pages will be prepared in manuscript.

Hour, Date, Place		Summary of Events and Information	Remarks and references to Appendices
NOEUX-les-MINES			
9th Octr. 1915	9.30 am.	Inspection by IIIrd Corps Commander. Battn. paraded & inspected by C.O.	
10th " "	9 am.	Church Parade (C of E) (Holy Communion 7 am)	
" "	10 "	Nonconformists	
" "	11.15 "	R.C.	
11th " "	9 am.	Attack practice at K.10.c (ref. 36B Sheet 1/40,000).	
" "	Afternoon	Inspection of arms, ammun., equipment &c by O.C. Companies.	
" "	4 to 6 pm.	Bathing "C" Coy. Draft of 6 Officers arrived from 3rd/23rd Br. Lon. Regt. — Lieuts H.E. Gaunt, R.D. Wood, 2/Lt. L. de B. Kelsey, S.J. Windows, E.S. Potter, R.D. Norman.	
12th Octr. 1915	a.m.	all rifles cleaned.	
" "	12 noon	" " inspected by Commanding Officer.	
TRENCHES	5.45 pm	Battn. paraded and marched to reserve trenches near LES BREBIS.	
13th " 1915	9 am.	Capt. H. Ruthven returned from leave. Battn. left trenches and marched to reserve trenches in PHILOSOPHE. (right flank on LENS-BETHUNE Road)	
14th " 1915		Draft of 48 other ranks arrived from Base.	
15th " 1915	7 pm.	Battn. relieved by 4th Bn. R.W.F. and marched to billets, MAZINGARBE	
16th " 1915	8.30 a.m.	New draft inspected by C.O. and M.O.	
" "	9.30 "	elementary drill and attack practice	
" "	5.30 pm.	Battn. marched to reserve trenches at G.16.d.2.2. relieving 21st. 18th L.R. (see British front line)	

Army Form C. 2118.

WAR DIARY
or
INTELLIGENCE SUMMARY
(Erase heading not required.)

Instructions regarding War Diaries and Intelligence Summaries are contained in F.S. Regs., Part II. and the Staff Manual respectively. Title pages will be prepared in manuscript.

Hour, Date, Place	Summary of Events and Information	Remarks and references to Appendices
TRENCHES		
16th Oct. 1915	Capt. C.F.H. Greenwood & 2/Lt. W.G. Newton (25th Bn. L.R - Artists Rifles) reported for duty, latter as Adjt.	
17th " 1915	Working party of 200 men digging communication trench	
18th " 1915	" " 200 " " " "	
19th " 1915	" " 200 " " " " (A & D Coys)	
20th " 1915	Remainder of Bn. marched to PHILOSOPHE and billeted	
PHILOSOPHE		
21st " 1915	B & C Companies } marched & marched to flagged course MAZINGARBE for attack practice.	
22nd " 1915 9 a.m.	B Coy. MG & signallers } marched to flagged course, MAZINGARBE for attack practice.	
9.10 "	C " " "	
9.20 "	A " " "	
9.30 "	D " " "	
23rd " 1915 10.15	Battn. practised attack at MAZINGARBE	
5 p.m.	A,B & C Coys in firing line, D Coy in support. marched to SECTION B.2. relieving 8th Bn. Lon. Regt (P.O.R.)	
SECTION B.2		
24th Oct. 1915	2 Casualties (1 killed, 1 wounded).	
25th " 1915	6 " (1 " 5 ") 2/Lt S.G. DOWNING returned to duty	
26th " 1915	12 " (2 " 10 ")	
	Lieut B.E. GRAY reported from B-ase for duty	

Army Form C. 2118.

WAR DIARY
or
INTELLIGENCE SUMMARY

(Erase heading not required.)

Instructions regarding War Diaries and Intelligence Summaries are contained in F. S. Regs., Part II. and the Staff Manual respectively. Title pages will be prepared in manuscript.

Hour, Date, Place		Summary of Events and Information	Remarks and references to Appendices
SECTION B 2.			
27th October 1915	6pm	Battn. relieved by 21st Bn. Lon Regt. Battn. in support.	
		2 Casualties (1 killed, 1 wounded).	
28th		4 " (1 " 3 ")	
29th 1915			
30th 1915		2/Lt C. A. Astley joined from Base.	
		3 Casualties (3 wounded).	
31st 1915		3 " (1 killed, 2 wounded).	

17/11/15.

William S. Newton
Lieut & Adjt.
for OC 23rd Bn: The London Regt. T.F.

142nd Inf. Bde.
47th Division.

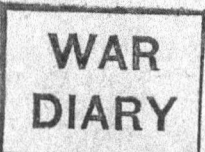

1/23rd LONDON REGT.

NOVEMBER

1915

WAR DIARY
or
INTELLIGENCE SUMMARY
(Erase heading not required.)

Army Form C. 2118.

Hour, Date, Place	Summary of Events and Information	Remarks and references to Appendices
SECTION B2.		
1st November 1915	Battalion in front line trenches having relieved 21st 1st London Regt. on 31st Octr.	
2nd 1915	Draft of 50 other ranks arrived from Base. Casualties 3 (1 Killed, 2 Wounded)	
3rd 1915	Casualties 7 (3 Killed, 4 wounded)	
4th 1915	Battn. relieved in front line by 24th Bn Lon Regt and returned to old German front line (Trentt Avenue) in support reserve.	
5th 1915	2/Lt R.D. Marsman to Trench mortar Course. Commanding Officer (Major T.G.W. Newman) proceeded on short leave to England	
6th 1915	2/Lt R. BULGIN returned from Bomb School. Battn. relieved in supp. reserve trenches by 17th Bn Lon Regt. Marched to PHILOSOPHÉ + billeted.	
PHILOSOPHÉ		
7th 1915 (Sunday)	Devoted to cleaning arms, equipment & clothing.	
8th	Inspection of rifles, equipment &c.	
	2 pm. Draft inspected by M.O. L'GAUTÉ to Bomb School.	
9th	Companies bathed at MAZINGARBE Barwen as follows. A Coy 6-8 am, B Coy 9-11 am, C Coy 11am - 1pm	
10th	2.15 pm 1st Rein. Grenadier Platoon handed under 2/Lt BULGIN for instruction.	
	6-8 am C Coy + M.G. at Baths, MAZINGARBE	
	9-11 " D " " "	
	11 am - 1 pm Grenadier Platoon " "	
	12 noon Inspection of billets by Commanding Officer. C Coy Lcpl 9 men Killed and 7 wounded by a shell which struck billet.	

WAR DIARY
or
INTELLIGENCE SUMMARY

(Erase heading not required.)

Army Form C. 2118.

Hour, Date, Place		Summary of Events and Information	Remarks and references to Appendices
PHILOSOPHE			
November 1915 11th	5.45 pm	Working party of 300 men provided for work on trench tramway under Capt. TOLERTON. 2/Lt J. WINDOWS to admitted to hospital.	
12th		Billets + billeting area thoroughly cleaned in anticipation of move. No 1136 Cpl. Lept Major R. HOXMAN, "A" Coy, awarded CROIX de GUERRE. Capt GREENWOOD On leave to England.	
13th	10 am	2nd Bn K.R.R.C. marched into PHILOSOPHE to work until evening to enter trenches.	
	12 noon	Battn. marched by half companies to NOEUX-les-MINES Rly Stn. + entrained for LOZINGHEM, arriving 5 pm + billeting.	
LOZINGHEM			
14th		Clothing + equipment thoroughly cleaned + overhauled. 2/Lt R.D. WOOD to Bomb School.	
	12 noon	Inspection of billets by Commanding Officer.	
15th	7.15-7.45 am	Physical Training.	
	9.30 am-12.30 Afternoon	Close order drill and manual under Coy arrangements. Devoted to cleaning up. Commanding officer returned from leave.	
16th	7.15-7.45 am	Physical Training.	
	9.30 am-12.30 pm	Close order drill. Inspection by Commanding Officer.	
	2-4 pm	Musketry instruction and Bayonet fighting.	
	3.30 pm	Reserve Stretcher Bearers instructed by Medical Officer.	
17th	7.15-7.45 am	Physical training.	
	9.30 am	Battalion route march. Right Half under Capt BRETT. Left half under Capt. RUTHVEN.	
18th	7.15-7.45 am	Physical training.	
	9.30-12.30 pm	Coys. drill + training. Sergts + Corpls. of A+B Coys. under Adjutant.	
	2-4 pm	Musketry instruction and Bayonet fighting.	

Army Form C. 2118.

WAR DIARY
or
INTELLIGENCE SUMMARY

(Erase heading not required.)

Instructions regarding War Diaries and Intelligence Summaries are contained in F. S. Regs, Part II. and the Staff Manual respectively. Title pages will be prepared in manuscript.

Hour, Date, Place	Summary of Events and Information	Remarks and references to Appendices
LOZINGHEM		
19th November 1915 7.15-7.45 am	Physical training.	
9.30 am	Kit inspection. All deficiencies noted & indented for. Sergts. & Corpls. of "C" "D" Coys under Adjutant for instruction	
20" 1915 7.15-7.45 am	Physical training.	
9.30 am	Battn route march. Lt R.D. WOOD returned from Bomb School.	
21st " 9.45 am	Church Parade. 2/Lt F.R. HONEYBALL to Bomb School.	
22nd " 7.15-7.45 "	Physical training.	
9.30 am	All men who joined since July exercised on Range	
9.30 "	All Corpls. under Adjutant for drill.	
23rd " 7.15-7.45 am	Physical training.	
9.45 am	1 N.C.O & 1 men from each Coy handed under Lt D J WARDLEY & marched to BETHUNE as fatigue party.	
3.30 pm	Inspection of Transport by O.C. 47" Divl. Train	
24" 7.15-7.45 am 9.30-10.30	Physical training. Class men & specifics Coy arrangements	
6.30 pm	Battn. handed for inspection by Field-Marshal Commanding-in-Chief. Lt.Col. 142 Inf Bde	
25" 7.15-7.45 am	Physical training.	
9.30 am	Battn. route march	
1.30 pm	C & D Coys	
2.15 "	A & B Coys & Transport paraded for baths at MARLES-les-MINES	

Army Form C. 2118.

WAR DIARY
or
INTELLIGENCE SUMMARY
(Erase heading not required.)

Instructions regarding War Diaries and Intelligence Summaries are contained in F. S. Regs., Part II. and the Staff Manual respectively. Title pages will be prepared in manuscript.

Hour, Date, Place	Summary of Events and Information	Remarks and references to Appendices
LOZINGHEM.		
26th Mar 1915 9.15-7.45 am	Physical training.	
10.30 am	30 NCOs + men from each Coy paraded + marched to Gen Holmes demonstration at c.12 a. b.3 (near ALLOUAGNE).	
2-3.30 pm	1 hr. squad drill, 1 hr. bayonet fighting. Dept of 19 NCOs from Base.	
27th Mar 1915.	Physical training.	
9.30 am-12.30 pm	Parade under Coy arrangements for musketry instruction + bayonet fighting. C.O. inspected Companies as follows:	
	A Coy 10 am	
	B " 10.30 "	
	C " 11 "	
	D " 11.30 "	
10 am	Men of draft medically examined.	
28th Mar 1915 9.15 am	Church Parade	
12 noon	C.O. inspected Transport.	
29" 1915	Physical training (breathing exercises).	
9.30-11 am	Close order + squad drill.	
11 am-12 noon	Musketry instruction.	
12-12.30 pm	Bayonet fighting.	
2-3 pm	Indict discipline. Attack practice + passing of orders.	
30"		
9.30-11 am	Manual exercises + close order drill.	
11-11.30 am	Extended order drill. Bayonet exercises	
2-3 pm	Lecture on Outposts (under Coy arrangements)	

A.G. Henderson
Lt.
for O.C. 23rd Bn The London Regt.

142nd Inf. Bde.
47th Division.

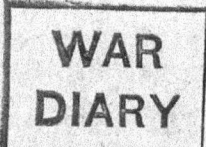

1/23rd LONDON REGT.

DECEMBER

1915

Army Form C. 2118.

WAR DIARY
or
INTELLIGENCE SUMMARY.
(Erase heading not required.)

Instructions regarding War Diaries and Intelligence Summaries are contained in F. S. Regs., Part II. and the Staff Manual respectively. Title pages will be prepared in manuscript.

Place	Date	Hour	Summary of Events and Information	Remarks and references to Appendices
LOZINGHEM	1915 Dec 1st	8.45 am	Battn paraded to take part in Divisional Route March. Battn at WITERNESS E for night.	
	2nd	8 am	" " and marched to LOZINGHEM, arriving at 2.30 p.m.	
	3rd	7.15-7.45 am	Physical training. 9.30-11 Manual exercise, close order Coy drill. 11-12 Extended order drill. 12-12.30 Bayonet fighting. 2-3 p.m. Lectures by O.C. Coys on Outposts, duties of sentries &c. 4 p.m. Lecture by Adjt to C.S.Ms & platoon Sergts. Lewis Gun Section formed under 2/Lt R.D. NORMAN.	
	4th	7.15- am	7.15 - in Physical training. 9.30 am Battn route march.	
	5th	7.30 am	Holy Communion. 9.15 Parade Service	
	6th	7.15 - 7.45 am	Physical Training. 9.30 am 4 men per Coy instructed in trench cooking. Battn instructed in wiring by 2/Lt A.B. GRAY	
	7th	7.15-7.45	Physical training. 9.30-11 {A+B Coys wiring practice a+B Extended order drill} 11-12.30 C+D Wiring practice 2-4 p.m. {C+D Extended order drill} Bathing at MARLES-les-MINES	
	8th	7.15-7.45	Physical training. 9.30-11 9 am Range practice for Lewis Gun Section, ALLOUGNE. A+B Coys. Practice in Outpost 11-12.30 A+B Coys - wiring practice 2-3 p.m. C+D " Wiring practice C+D Outpost duties. Lectures by O.C. Coys. on Outpost duties. Bde Shooting Comp. at LABEUVRIERE.	
	9th	7.15-7.45	Physical training. 9.30-10.30 Close order drill. 10-30 - 12. Outpost duties. 12-12.30 p.m. Bayonet fighting. 2-3 pm Lectures by O.C. Coys. on Outpost duties.	

Army Form C. 2118.

WAR DIARY
or
INTELLIGENCE SUMMARY.
(Erase heading not required.)

Instructions regarding War Diaries and Intelligence Summaries are contained in F. S. Regs., Part II. and the Staff Manual respectively. Title pages will be prepared in manuscript.

Place	Date 1915	Hour	Summary of Events and Information	Remarks and references to Appendices
LOZINGHEM	Dec 10th	7.15-7.45 am	Physical training. 9.30 - 12. m. Close order drill. Coy. Dugout practice. 2-3 pm Demonstration by M.O. on use of anti-frostbite grease.	
	11th	—	Physical training. Commanding Officer inspected Bn. from 10.15 - 11 am. Route march by Companies.	
	12th	8 am and 10 am	Bomb throwing for all ranks not used to Mills Bomb. 9.15 am. Church Parade.	
	13th	7.15-7.45	Physical training. Lecture by Bde. Major on Trench routine to all Officers, C.S.Ms + platoon Sergts.	
		9.30	Cleaning of arms + equipment. 11 am Fitting of equipment. 11.30. Application of anti-frostbite grease. Issue of second tube helmet to all ranks.	
	14th	8.45 am	Bn. paraded + marched to LILLERS, entrained to NOEUX-les-MINES + marched to VAUDRICOURT.	
VAUDRICOURT	15th	"	" SAILLY LABOURSE + billeted	
		10.15	Battn. entered Trenches D.1, relieving Batln. of 15th Division. "A" firing line, "B" support "C" Reserve, "D" Coy. remaining at SAILLY LABOURSE	
D1	16th	4 pm	Adjpo and "A" Coy returned to SAILLY LABOURSE. 24th Bn. L.R. took over front line. "B" Coy joined "C" in reserve in LANCASHIRE Trench. Casualties: 1 wounded. Service Coy. 3rd Lon. Regt attached for duty.	
	19th	8 am	Bn. relieved 24th Bn L.R. in D.1. "A" Coy + 3rd Lon. Coy (attached) firing line, B, C support, D in reserve Hdqrs. in CANNON ST. off QUARRY ALLEY.	
	20th	—	Casualties: 1 Killed (Pte RADMALL) 2 Wounded. C + D Coys. replaced 3rd Lon. Coy. in front line. 3rd Lon. Coy. in reserve.	
	23rd	6.30 am	Bn. relieved by 18th Bn. Lon. Regt. + marched to billets in SAILLY LABOURSE. Casualty: 1 Wounded.	

Army Form C. 2118.

WAR DIARY
or
INTELLIGENCE SUMMARY.
(Erase heading not required.)

Instructions regarding War Diaries and Intelligence Summaries are contained in F.S. Regs., Part II. and the Staff Manual respectively. Title pages will be prepared in manuscript.

Place	Date 1915	Hour	Summary of Events and Information	Remarks and references to Appendices
SAILLY LABOURSE	Decr. 24th	3.30 P.M. 4.30 "	Inspections of arms and equipment. A, B, C, Coys + Lewis Gun paraded for tests at Force No 6 LABOURSE D + 3rd Lon Companies " " " "	
	25th	7 am 7.30 "	Holy Communion. 9.15 Parade Service. " " " "	
	26th	11 am	R.C. service in French Church.	
	27th	8.45am	Bn paraded and marched by half Coys. to NOYELLES, and HULLUCH	
NOYELLES	28th		Inspections by O.C. Coys and application of anti-frostbite grease. Coy Commanders reconnoitred Sector C.1	
	29th	3.45 am	A, C + D Coys paraded and marched to CURLY CRESCENT (dugouts) relieving 22nd B.n L.R. B Coy + 3rd Lon Coy in VERMELLES.	
	30th	4.30 P.M.	In consequence of Germans springing 5 mines in HAIRPIN, C Coy were sent to support 22nd Bn L.R. and "B" Coy moved up to CURLY CRESCENT. 1 Killed (Grenadier)	
	31st	2 am	Battn. relieved 22nd Bn L.R. in Sector C.2. Bn. all in front line, 3rd Lon Coy in support. Casualties: 2 Killed (Grenadiers).	

W. J. Newton
Lt + Adjt.
for O.C. 23rd Bn. The London Regt.

Army Form C. 2118.

23 London Regt

WAR DIARY
or
INTELLIGENCE SUMMARY.
(Erase heading not required.)

Instructions regarding War Diaries and Intelligence Summaries are contained in F.S. Regs., Part II and the Staff Manual respectively. Title pages will be prepared in manuscript.

Hour, Date, Place		Summary of Events and Information	Remarks and references to Appendices
SECTION C 2			
1st Jan 1916		Casualties – 2 wounded.	
4th " "	8 a.m.	Bn. relieved by Cavalry Division (3rd Battn.) marched to NOYELLES had breakfast, marched to SAILLY LABOURSÉ, which motor lorries conveyed Bn. to HOUCHIN.	
5th " "	3.30 p.m.	Bn. marched to LES BREBIS and billeted. Lt. F. ENTWISLE rejoined from Base.	
LES BREBIS			
6th " "		Parties under Coy. arrangements	
7th " "			
8th " "		Bn. marched to MAROC in support: HdQrs. A.B. & C Coys in S. MAROC. "D" and 3rd Bn. (under Major KEMBLE) in N. MAROC	
DOUBLE CRASSIER.			
10th " "		Bn. relieved 24th Bn. L.R. in but sector C (MAROC) DOUBLE CRASSIER A.B. D + 2 platoons 3rd Bn in Coy firing line; D + 2 platoons 3rd Bn in support. HdQrs. in O.G.1. Casualty: 1 wounded. 7 Cadets attached for 48 hrs instruction.	
11th " "		" " "	
12th " "		Bn. relieved by 21st Bn Lon Regt	
14th " "		Bn. in support at S. MAROC (B + C in N. MAROC).	
15th " "		" marched to BRAQUEMONT in evening of 16th	
16		Cleaning rifles and equipment	
LES BREBIS			
16th " "	8.30 a.m.	Working party of 2 officers + 130 men (3rd Bn) on road from Fosse 2 to	

Army Form C. 2118.

WAR DIARY
or
INTELLIGENCE SUMMARY.
(Erase heading not required.)

Instructions regarding War Diaries and Intelligence Summaries are contained in F.S. Regs., Part II. and the Staff Manual respectively. Title pages will be prepared in manuscript.

Hour, Date, Place	Summary of Events and Information	Remarks and references to Appendices
BRAQUEMONT		
18th January 1916. 12.30 pm	Similar party (23rd Bn.) relieved final party.	
19th " 10.30 am	Lecture by Major SAMUEL, 3rd bn. to battalion officers & N.C.O.'s on sniping.	
" 8.15–9.15	B Coy bathed	
" 9.15–10.15	C " "	
" 10.15–11.15	D " "	
" 11.30 – noon	L.G. section	
20th " 8–9	Grenadiers bathing	
" 9–9.45	Signallers & Scouts	
" 9.45–10.30	"A" Coy bathing.	
" 3.50 pm	Bn. paraded & marched to Right half section, LOOS sector to relieve 7th Bn. L.R. R B C & D firing line, 2 platoons 3rd in support, 2 platoons in reserve billets at LOOS. Hqrs. in POST OFFICE, LOOS.	
	*Coy. 7th Lincolns Regt. attached for instruction.	
	Casualties: 1 wounded.	
LOOS		
22nd Jany 1916	2 killed, 4 wounded.	
23rd "		
24th "	3rd bn. Coy relieved C & D in firing line. C in reserve billets in LOOS, D in support.	
25th "	Casualties: 3 wounded	
26th "	Casualties: 2/Lt. G.C. Turner wounded, 1 O.R. wounded.	
27th "	" 1 OR KILLED (1820, Pte MILLS R.A.)	
	Capt. C.A. BRETT	

WAR DIARY
or
INTELLIGENCE SUMMARY.
(Erase heading not required.)

Army Form C. 2118.

Instructions regarding War Diaries and Intelligence Summaries are contained in F.S. Regs., Part II. and the Staff Manual respectively. Title pages will be prepared in manuscript.

Hour, Date, Place	Summary of Events and Information	Remarks and references to Appendices
LOOS 28th January 1916	Battalion relieved by 10th Bn Lon Regt and marched to BRAQUEMONT	
BRAQUEMONT 29th January 1916 9 a.m.	Working party (C & D Companies) for work at Fosse N° 11 LES BREBIS.	
30th 9.30 a.m.	Parade Service. Rifles overhauled by Divl. Armourer Sergt.	
31st 7 a.m.	Working party of 100 men under 2/Lt R.G. Williams for work on new road from Fosse N° 11 to LES BREBIS.	
8 – 12 noon	Bathing by Companies at Fosse N° 11 Dupont.	

31-1-16

A.J. Henderson
Lt. Adjt.
for O.C. 23rd Bn The London Regt

404.

23 London Regt
Feb
Vol XII

WAR DIARY or INTELLIGENCE SUMMARY

Army Form C. 2118.

(Erase heading not required.)

Hour, Date, Place	Summary of Events and Information	Remarks and references to Appendices
BRAQUEMONT 1st February 1916	Bn. moved to S. MAROC, relieving 7th Bn. L.R. in support. A, B & D in S. MAROC, C & 3rd Ln Cny in N. MAROC (Capt D.C.L. WARD in Command)	
3rd " 1916	Bn. relieved 24th Bn L.R. 3rd Ldn in firing line, D Coy support, B.C. & A in reserve.	
6th "	Casualties: 1 wounded.	
7th "	Draft of 77 O.R. under 2/Lt L.G. Chivete joined Bn. and found working party for carrying skeevers-de-frise to front line.	
9th "	Bn. relieved by 20th Bn L.R. & marched to trenches @ BRAQUEMONT.	
11th BRAQUEMONT	Bathed at Fosse No 1. Dufort Rifles of Bn. inspected by Dist. Armourer.	
12th February 1916 8.15am	Working party of 1 Off + 100 other ranks on new road to LES BREBIS.	
12.15 pm	" " 10 " " relieved first party	
13th " 10 am	Church Parade 1 Off + 25 O.R. attached 173rd Tunnelling Coy R.E.	
14th " 11.30 am	Bn. marched to NOEUX-LES-MINES, entrained to LILLERS and marched to RAIMBERT in Army Reserve.	
15th "	Bn. marched to new billets at BURBURE.	
16th " 6.15 pm	Working party of 1 Off + 50 other ranks to Bac Haque.	
19th " 9	C.O. inspection	
20th " 6.30 am	Working party of 1 Off + 50 other ranks to Bac Algre.	
" 9.30	Church Parade.	

WAR DIARY
or
INTELLIGENCE SUMMARY

(Erase heading not required.)

Army Form C. 2118.

Instructions regarding War Diaries and Intelligence Summaries are contained in F. S. Regs., Part II. and the Staff Manual respectively. Title pages will be prepared in manuscript.

Hour, Date, Place		Summary of Events and Information	Remarks and references to Appendices
BURBURE			
21st February 1916.		Bn. bathed at MARLES-les-MINES.	
22nd	7.50 am	Paraded and marched to ERNY ST JULIEN in severe snowstorm.	
24th	"	Training	
25th	8.30 am	Brigade "	
26th	"	Battn. "	
27th		Church Parade under Coy arrangements.	
		Brigade training postponed owing to frost & snow.	
28th		Scheme carried out in conjunction with 24th Bn. L.R.	
29th	8.50 am	Bn. paraded and marched back to BURBURE	

3rd March 1916.

M. J. Alerton. 2t. Adj.
for O.C. 23rd Bn. The London Regt. T.F.

WAR DIARY or INTELLIGENCE SUMMARY

Army Form C. 2118.

Hour, Date, Place	Summary of Events and Information	Remarks and references to Appendices
BURBURE		
1st March 1916	Route March at Five Road AUCHEL. Note went to Mellicourt for wiring practice.	
2nd " " 9-12.45am	Battalion practiced Bayonet Drill. Outpost scheme not attended later.	
7th " " 5.0 am	Battalion moved to BARLIN, relieving Fusil. Compts. Billets taken over in a dirty condition.	
BARLIN		
8th " " 8.45 am	Battalion marched to COUPIGNY to clean out huts and COUPIGNY Lines generally after being evacuated by the Forresters.	
9th " "	Battalion moved to Billets in COUPIGNY Huts, by parties at the following times. 9am, 9.15am, 9.30am, 9.45am, 10.0am, 10.15am	
COUPIGNY		
10 & March 1916 9-10 am	Cleaning of huts and lines generally.	
10-12.30, 2-4 pm		
" " 5.0 pm	Battalion paraded for night working party, returning at 2.0 am	
11th March 1916 5.0 pm	Battalion paraded for night working party, returning at 2.30 am	
13th " " 7-7.30 am	Physical training under by Officers.	
" " 9.30 am	Bn. paraded for Outpost scheme under by Officers.	
14th " " 5.0 pm	Bn. paraded for night working party, returning at 1.30 am	
16th " " 6.30 am	Battalion paraded and moved to Billets at ESTREE CAUCHIE	
17th " " 7.45 am	Battalion paraded for working party, and returned at 3.30 pm	

Army Form C. 2118.

WAR DIARY
or
INTELLIGENCE SUMMARY
(Erase heading not required.)

Instructions regarding War Diaries and Intelligence Summaries are contained in F. S. Regs., Part II. and the Staff Manual respectively. Title pages will be prepared in manuscript.

Hour, Date, Place	Summary of Events and Information	Remarks and references to Appendices
18 March 1916 7.30am 9.0am	Physical training under Coy Officers. Battalion parade for practicing Artillery formations	
19th March 1916 11.0 am	Battalion paraded for inspection in practice dam the Helmets.	
20 " "	Battn Bathed at FRESNICOURT.	
21st " " 10.45 am	Battalion moved to Billets at Gouy SERVINS, relieving the 8th Bn. the Lon Regt.	
22nd " " 8.30 am	Half Battn paraded for working party, returning at 1.30 pm.	
" 1.15 pm	Half " " " " 6.0 pm.	
23rd " 5.30 pm	Battalion " " " " 12.30 am.	
24th " 5.15 "	Battalion " " " " 1.30 am.	
25th " 5.15 "	Battalion " " " " 2.0 am.	
26th " 11-12.30 am 5.15 pm	Men got well rubbed with whale oil and clean socks put on. Half Battalion paraded for working party.	
27th " 12.35 pm	Battalion paraded and marched to Cambrin, relieving the 1st Battalion Lon Regt.	

1st April.

F. Walsh
Lt & Adjt
for O.C. 23rd Lon Regt.

47
42

1/23 London Regt

Vol XIV

April

16th

Army Form C. 2118.

WAR DIARY
or
INTELLIGENCE SUMMARY.
(Erase heading not required.)

Instructions regarding War Diaries and Intelligence Summaries are contained in F. S. Regs, Part II. and the Staff Manual respectively. Title pages will be prepared in manuscript.

Place	Date	Hour	Summary of Events and Information	Remarks and references to Appendices
LORETTE HEIGHTS	2/4/16	—	Bn. relieved by 20th Bn. The London Regt. & marched to VILLERS AU BOIS	
	3/4/16	—	" marched to billets at MAISNIL BOUCHÉ.	
	4/4/16	10 am	" Bathed at FRESNICOURT	
		6 pm	Lecture by Corps Commander at GRAND SERVINS. to Officers only.	
	5/4/16	3 pm	Manual exercises	
		9–10 am		
		10–11	Outpost duties. 11–3.45 medical inspection by Companies.	
		6.15 pm	Bn. paraded as Working Party, returning at 1 AM 6th.	
	6/4/16		Lewis Gun & Bombing instruction	
		6 pm	Working Party 100 men (25 per Coy) under 2/Lt Johnson	
	7/4/16	8.30 am		
		9.30	Bn. marched to BOUVIGNY HUTS, relieving 15th Bn. Lon. Regt.	
	8/4/16	7 pm	" " LORETTE HEIGHTS trenches, relieving 4th Bn. London Regt. (Bn. in reserve trenches).	
	14/4/16	7.30	" relieved by 20th Bn. Lon. Regt. : 1 Coy at VILLERS AU BOIS, 3 Coys. at CARENCY. 1 Wounded.	
15–18/4/16		9 pm	" Found working parties each night.	
	19/4/16		" marched to billets at VERDREL.	
	20/4/16	7.45 am	Working party of 100 O.R. under 2/Lt CHORCHER & IRESON for work with 138th Coy R.E.	
		4 pm	Bn. moved to billets at FRESNICOURT	

Army Form C. 2118.

WAR DIARY
or
INTELLIGENCE SUMMARY.
(Erase heading not required.)

Instructions regarding War Diaries and Intelligence Summaries are contained in F. S. Regs., Part II. and the Staff Manual respectively. Title pages will be prepared in manuscript.

Place	Date	Hour	Summary of Events and Information	Remarks and references to Appendices
FRESNICOURT	21/4/16	12.00 / 7-9	Bn. bathed.	
	22/2/16	11 am / 6.30 pm	C.O. inspected Bn. 3.30 pm. Bn. inspected by B.G.C. Working party of 100 men under 1st Johnson & Entwistle.	
	23/4/16	11.30	Draft of 91 men joined from Inf. Training School Parade Service. Working Party of 100 men under 2/Lt Trivial & Whalley. (6.30 pm)	
		2.30	Medical Inspection of Draft.	
	24/4/16	9-12.45 am / 6.30	Coy parades for drill & musketry, Physical training, bombing & Bn. Drill Working party of 100 men under 2/Lt Williams & Norman.	
	25/4/16	9-12.45	Same as 24/4/16. Working Party of 50 men under 2/Lt H.K. Pearle.	
	26/4/16	9 am	Bn. Drill.	
		4 pm	Paraded & marched to BOUVIGNY HUTS, relieving 22nd Bn. London Regt.	
BOUVIGNY	27/4/16	9-1	Bombing, L.G. & musketry instruction: bayonet fighting 100 men under Lt Payne, working party.	
	28/4/16		" " " 100 " " 2/Lt Williams & Norman – do –	
	29/4/16		—	
			{ 25 " " 2/Lt Bulgin	
			{ 75 " " Lt Wardley, a Lieut.	
			{ 25	
			{ 75 " " 2/Lt Honeyball	
	30/4/16	am / 11	Major T.C. Hargreaves reported from England. Church Parade.	

W.S. Penton Lt & Adjt.
for O.C. 23rd Bn The London Regt.

1/23 London R⁴
Vol 15

WAR DIARY
or
INTELLIGENCE SUMMARY
(Erase heading not required.)

Army Form C. 2118.

Instructions regarding War Diaries and Intelligence Summaries are contained in F.S. Regs., Part II. and the Staff Manual respectively. Title pages will be prepared in manuscript.

Hour, Date, Place	Summary of Events and Information	Remarks and references to Appendices
BOUVIGNY		
1st May 1916. 11.10 PM	Bn. marched to VILLERS AU BOIS (H.Q. & A Coy) and CARENCY (B.C. & D Coy) relieving 8th Bn. L.R.	
7.30 P.M.	Bn. marched to "C" Subsector SOUCHEZ Sector, relieving 15th Bn L.R.	
SOUCHEZ SECTOR		
3rd	"C" front line, A & B in QUARRIES, "D" Coy reserve. Casualties: 4 wounded	
4th	" 3 "	
5th	" — "B" front line, A & C in QUARRIES, "D" reserve	
6th	"	
7th	A Coy front line, B & C in QUARRIES, D Coy in reserve	
8th 11 P.M.	Bn. relieved by 17th Bn L.R. & marched to VILLERS AU BOIS.	
9th 2 "	" marched to VERDREL and billeted.	
VERDREL		
May 1916	Kit inspections, cleaning up.	
9pm	Working party of 50 men (C & D) under 2/Lt Wardley & 2/Lt Trainer	
9pm	2/Lt R.G. THOMSON reported for duty.	
10th " 9am-1pm	Drill, Bombing, Smoke Helmet Drill, Physical training, musketry.	
" " 12 noon	"	
11th " 1.30 pm	Bn. paraded & marched to FRESNICOURT for address by Corps Commander	
	Working party of 100 men under 2/Lts WARDLEY and 2/Lt THOMSON	
12th 9am-6.30pm	Battn. bathed at FRESNICOURT. Coys in practised manoeuvres in BOIS D'OLHAIN.	
	Musketry. L.G. instructional class.	
13th 9.am	Bn. parade (less B Coy - musketry)	
9.30 am		

WAR DIARY or INTELLIGENCE SUMMARY

Army Form C. 2118.

Hour, Date, Place	Summary of Events and Information	Remarks and references to Appendices
VERDREL		
14th May 1916. 10 P.M.	D, A & C Coys. marched to CARENCY) into trench reserve
" " 11.30 p.m.	H.Q. & B. Coy. " " VILLERS AU BOIS) relieving 17th Bn. L.R.
	5 men rejoined Bn. from G.H.Q.	
VILLERS.	Orders received for 1 Lewis Gun team to be attached 24th Bn. L.R.	
16th May 1916	2/Lt H.E. GAUTE and 2 O.R. to BASE for recruit training	
	Working party of 50 men to Right Subsection	
17th "	" " 50 " " Centre . 1 O.R. wounded	
18th "	" " 50 (carrying)	
20th "	Casualty. 1 O.R. wounded.	
21st "	Bn. bathed at VILLERS	
22nd " 10.30 a.m.	Parade service.	
" 5.40 p.m.	Received orders to be ready to move at 1 hrs notice, owing to heavy shelling by enemy of VIMY RIDGE.	
" 11.30	Bn. moved to MAISTRE LINE, relieving 15th Bn. L.R. who advanced	
" 12.30 A.M.	placed under orders of 140th Inf. Bde. and moved up to support in ~~Villy~~ CABARET ROUGE.	
	2 Coys attached 24th Bn. , 2 Coys to 21st Bn. as carrying parties ~~left~~	
23rd. 1.30 A.M.	Bn. returned to CARENCY.	
6. P.M.	moved into MAISTRE Line, + then up CABARET ROAD.	
	2 Coys attached 24th Bn. LR. C+D atts 21st Bn LR for carrying	

Army Form C. 2118.

WAR DIARY
or
INTELLIGENCE SUMMARY.
(Erase heading not required.)

Instructions regarding War Diaries and Intelligence Summaries are contained in F. S. Regs., Part II. and the Staff Manual respectively. Title pages will be prepared in manuscript.

Place	Date	Hour	Summary of Events and Information	Remarks and references to Appendices
	23/5/16		Owing to artillery barrage, no carrying done as nothing was asked for. Bn. spent night 23/24th in BAJOLLE line. Bombers under Lt BULGIN attached to 24th Bn. L.R. and L.G. section u/L WILLIAMS took part in the assault.	
	24/5/16	a.m.	relieved 21st Bn. L.R. in CARENCY Section: A, C + D, front line, B (with A Cy 22nd L.R.) reserve. 24th Bn. on our right, 20th Bn. on our left.	
	26/5/16	pm	Bn. relieved by 2/South Staffs Regt. and marched to VILLERS AU BOIS.	
	26/5/16	2.30pm	marched to OURTON, arriving at 8 P.M.; marching past Corps Commander en route.	
	27/5/16		Cleaning up, rifles inspected & all deficiencies indented for. Total casualties period 21-26/5: 5 killed, 1 missing, 25 wounded.	
OURTON	28/5/16	A.M. 10.30	Parade Service.	
		P.M. 2.40	Inspection + address by G.O.C. 1st Army.	
	29/5/16	9 AM	Bombing, Signalling, Coy. training in close order drill, bayonet fighting &c. Lt Greenwood 28th Bn. L.R.	
	28/5/16		Draft of 32 men arrived. Also draft of 40 men of 2/3rd Bn. L.R. (R.F.) 9 officers joined 29/5.	
	30/5/16	9 PM	Training as previous day. Draft of 24 men arrived.	
	31/5/16		1 Officer reported. Training under Coy arrangements. "A" Cy on range.	
		8 P.M. 8-10	Night work for D Cy.	

W McMahon
For O.C. 23rd Bn The London Regt.

142   47

1/23 London Regt

Vol XIII

47

1/23 London Regt
Vol 16

WAR DIARY
or
INTELLIGENCE SUMMARY
(Erase heading not required.)

Army Form C. 2118.

Hour, Date, Place	Summary of Events and Information	Remarks and references to Appendices
OURTON.		
1st June 1916 6.30 am	Squad drill musketry	
9.30-1pm	Coy drill re "B" Coy on range. 2/Lt WILLIAMS, R.G., in charge.	
8-10 pm	Night work "C" Coy	
2nd June 1916	As yesterday	
am 9-1 pm	"C" Coy on range. 1 pm "D" Coy on range	
8-10 pm	B Coy on night work.	
3rd " 9 am	Bn. parade. Practice Gas helmets carried.	
4th " 11.45	Church parade. Capt. G.E. PALMER, 2/3rd Bn. Ln Regt (R.F.) reported	
5th " 6.30-7.30	Early Parade.	
9 am-12.30	Coy parades for fire control, target indicators, double helmet drill	
2.30	All NCO's & Rifle under QM for guard mounting instruction.	
4.30 pm	Bn. marched to BRUAY to attend performance of Div Concert Party.	
6th " 6.30-7.15	Coy + Detachment training	
9 am	Bn. (less "Specialists") parade.	
" 8.30 am-7 pm	Bathing at OURTON.	
7th " 9 am	Bn. Training	
11.30	Transport inspected by Brig Genl. F. LEWIS, Comdg 141 Bde.	
	Battalion re-armed with short M.L.E rifle	

Army Form C. 2118.

WAR DIARY
or
INTELLIGENCE SUMMARY

(Erase heading not required.)

Instructions regarding War Diaries and Intelligence Summaries are contained in F. S. Regs., Part II. and the Staff Manual respectively. Title pages will be prepared in manuscript.

Hour, Date, Place		Summary of Events and Information	Remarks and references to Appendices
OURTON			
8th June 1916	8.30 a.m.	Battalion training.	
9th "	8.30	" " (A & B Coys)	
	3.30	"C" Coy on range (Lewis Demonstration at Divl Bomb School.)	
10th "	8.30	Bn Training (A & C Coys)	
	8.30	"B" Coy on range. "D" Coy musketry instruction under Coy. arrangements	
	4 pm	All Battalion Officers attended demonstration at Divl Gas School.	
11th "	11.15 a.m.	Parade Service	
	1.30 PM	Battn inspected by Lord Mayor of LONDON	
12th "	6.30-7.30	Interior economy. 2/Lt W.A. SOEVEN joined from Base	
	9 am	Bn paraded for route march	
	6.30 pm	200 O.R. under Capt D.C.C. WARD proceeded by motor lorries to BOUVIGNY for working party.	
13th "	6.30 AM	Battn marched to BOUVIGNY WOODS. Weather very wet & roads heavy.	
BOUVIGNY WOODS		Working Party of 200 O.R.	
14th "		" " 90	
	11 PM	Tanno pans procured & kept in accordance with 1st Army Orders.	
15th "		Working " " " under Coy Bombing.	
		Inspection of arms, equipment & Coy Bombing.	
		50 O.R. under Lt F ENTWISLE proceeded working party.	
17th "	NOON	Bn. marched to ANGRES 1 Section relieved 1st Bn Lon Regt (L.S.R.)	
		C. B. A. (right half of firing line) D Coy support	

1247 W 3299 200,000 (E) 8/14 J.B.C. & A. Forms/C. 2118/11.

Army Form C. 2118.

WAR DIARY
or
INTELLIGENCE SUMMARY
(Erase heading not required.)

Instructions regarding War Diaries and Intelligence Summaries are contained in F. S. Regs., Part II. and the Staff Manual respectively. Title pages will be prepared in manuscript.

Hour, Date, Place	Summary of Events and Information	Remarks and references to Appendices
ANGRES I Section. 21st June 1916.	Bn. relieved by 20th Bn. London Regt. Casualty 1 O.R. wounded. marched to BOUVIGNY WOODS.	
22 " " 9 P.M.	Interior economy. Bn. furnished HERSIN 9am - 5pm. Carrying party 11 Officers & 75 O.R.	
25 " 1916 9.15 P.M.	Bn. relieved 16th Bn. London Regt. in LORETTE SPUR. Disposition:- "C" Coy night "D" support (2 platoons) "D" Coy centre (2 platoons) "B" Coy left. A Coy detached posts at R.34.c.- Bombers in ABLAIN.	
27 " 1916	Bombers moved up to support (MAISTRE Line).	
30 " 1916 pm.	Bn. relieved by 9th Bn. London Regt. and returned to BOUVIGNY WOODS.	
2nd July 1916.		W[?] Mahon for O.C. 23rd Battn. The London Regt.

1247 W 3299 200,000 (E) 8/14 J.B.C. & A. Forms/C. 2118/11.

142nd Brigade.
47th Division.

1/23rd BATTALION

LONDON REGIMENT

JULY 1916

Army Form C. 2118.

1/23rd Batt. London Regt.

Vol 17

WAR DIARY
or
INTELLIGENCE SUMMARY.
(Erase heading not required.)

Instructions regarding War Diaries and Intelligence Summaries are contained in F.S. Regs., Part II and the Staff Manual respectively. Title pages will be prepared in manuscript.

Hour, Date, Place	Summary of Events and Information	Remarks and references to Appendices
BOUVIGNY WOODS.		
1st July 1916. a.m.	Interior economy, Kit cleaning etc.	
12 noon	Gas lecture by M.O. to all Officers	
8 P.M.	Working party of 2 Officers & 100 men	
2.30 p.m.	Commanding Officer's parade - marching order inspection.	
2nd July 1916. 11 a.m.	Divine Service. Gas lectures by Coy. & Detachment Commanders.	
3rd July 1916.	Bn. relieved 20th Bn. London Regt. in ANGRES I Sub-Sector. A, B & C in firing line (Right to Left) "D" in support. Draft of 270 N.C.O.s and men arrived from Base. Wounded 1 O.R. Casualties.	2/Lt A.J. HARMAN + 11 O.R. (7 on duty). 1856 Pte W. SOPER, killed.
4th "	"	
5th "	"	
6th "	"	
7th "	"	
8th "	"	
9/10th	Bn. relieved by 21st Bn. Lon. Regt. A.D., A & B Coys. moved to BULLY GRENAY, C & D remaining in MECHANICS TRENCH in support.	
10th 10 a.m.	Coy. Bombers of "A" Coy. marched to Bde. ground at HERSIN for practice.	

WAR DIARY
or
INTELLIGENCE SUMMARY.
(Erase heading not required.)

Army Form C. 2118.

Hour, Date, Place	Summary of Events and Information	Remarks and references to Appendices
BULLY GRENAY		
July 11th 1916 8.30 am / 1 pm	Bathing for A +B Coy at BULLY	
12th 8-12 am	C +D " "	
"	Coy Bombers of "B" Coy at Bde ground, HERSIN, for practice.	
13th	" " " " " "	
14th	" " " " " "	
15th a.m.	Refitting parades for boots + clothing.	
15th 4.30 pm	Bn. marched to FOSSE 10, SAINS-EN-GOHELLE, relieving How E Bn. R.N.D.	
"	Bn. marched to BOUVIGNY WOODS, relieving 15th Bn. London Regt (C.S.R).	
16th 10 A.M.	Divine Service.	
" 5.30 P.M.	Bn. paraded + marched to SOUCHEZ SECTOR (VIMY) relieving 1st Bn The Kings. A Coy Right, B Coy Left, Firing line, D Coy support, "C" Coy reserve. 22nd L.R. on left, 6th Lan. Regt on right.	
"	Casualties. 4 killed, 8 wounded. 2/Lts E. WARREN & J.H.S. HUNT joined from Base and from 15th Bn. Lon. Regt. respectively.	
18th	Draft of 65 O.R. arrived from Base.	
"	3 killed (2 D. of Wounds) & 5 wounded. (O.R)	
20th	"B" and "C" Coy changed over.	
21st	Casualties. 1 O.R. killed.	
22nd		
23rd		

WAR DIARY
or
INTELLIGENCE SUMMARY.
(Erase heading not required.)

Army Form C. 2118.

Hour, Date, Place	Summary of Events and Information	Remarks and references to Appendices
SOUCHEZ Secty.		
24th July 1916.	Bn. relieved by 21st Bn. The London Regt. and marched to VILLERS AU BOIS in Brigade reserve.	
25th " 1916 10am–3pm	Bathing at VILLERS AU BOIS	
VILLERS AU BOIS		
26th " 1916	Lt. ENTWISLE & Permanent Working Party, detached on 15th June 1916, rejoined Bn.	
9 am	Men of last 2 drafts (3 + 10 (7/1/16) inspected by Brig. Genl. Cuerly 142nd Inf. Bde.	
9.15 "	Capt. Bowden & Bn. Bombers practice in bombing pit nr Chateau de la HAIE	
27th " 9 – 11.30 AM	Bathing for P.W.R. and Dugout squads.	
" 9.15 am.	Bombers at bombing pit.	
28th " 12 noon	Bn. paraded and marched to OURTON; dinner en route. Arrived 7 PM	
OURTON		
29th " 11.30 am	Commanding Officer's inspection – marching order.	
" 3.30	" " " of Transport.	
30th " 3.30 P.M.	Bn. paraded and marched to AVERDOINGT; breakfast on road. Arrived 9.30 A.M.	
AVERDOINGT.		
31st	Musketry & bayonet instruction under Coy arrangements.	

M.B. Newton
Lt. Ady
for O.C. 1/23rd Bn. The London Regt.

142nd Brigade.
47th Division.

———————

1/23rd BATTALION

LONDON REGIMENT

AUGUST 1 9 1 6

WAR DIARY
or
INTELLIGENCE SUMMARY.
(Erase heading not required.)

Army Form C. 2118.

Vol 18

Hour, Date, Place	Summary of Events and Information	Remarks and references to Appendices
AUERDOINGT. August 1st 1916.		
10 a.m.	Company attachment instruction in musketry, gas helmet drill, extended order, etc.	
REMAISNIL.		
5.30 p.m.	Battn. marched to REMAISNIL. — 16 miles — resting Bn. at 7 p.m. at MAGNICOURT.	
2 — 2 a.m.	Battn. reached REMAISNIL.	
3. 8.30 a.m.	Route march — 5 miles — by Companies. Gas lecture for N.C.Os. at 11 a.m. Draft of 34 men arrived.	
2 p.m.	Officers reconnoitring.	
BERNATRE.		
4. 4.55 a.m.	Battn. marched to BERNATRE. 9 miles — arrived at 11 a.m.	
5. 5 a.m.	Battn. march to ST. RIQUIER. — 10 miles. Arrived at 11 a.m. MAJOR HARGREAVES returned for duty from England.	
ST. RIQUIER.		
6. 6 — 7 a.m.	Phys. training. 9 a.m. Battn. training. 6.15 p.m. Voluntary service. 11.30 " Brigade church parade.	
7. 6 a.m.	Bayt. fighting. 8 a.m. Battalion training — extended order, etc. Half hour platoon drill B.B.O. — Remainder digging at Battn. afternoon under Coy arrangements.	
5.30 p.m.	Band of 1/21st Lan.Regt. commenced nightly concert in Place. Capt. J.W. JORDAN, R.A.M.C. reported for duty. Companies dined alongside cellars —	
8. 5.45 a.m.	Physical drill. Battn. training. Yeatow B.B.S.O. — The attack, extending, formations, etc.	A. Blue B. Green C. Red D. Yellow
7.30		
9. 5.45 a.m.	Half hour Physical drill. 7.45 Battalion training in attack. Lewis gun instruction for officers, NCOs. 3.30 Musketry under Company arrangements. Remainder digging for A.P.B. Coy. trenches trial bombs.	

Army Form C. 2118.

INTELLIGENCE SUMMARY.
(Erase heading not required.)

Instructions regarding War Diaries and Intelligence Summaries are contained in F.S. Regs., Part II and the Staff Manual respectively. Title pages will be prepared in manuscript.

Hour, Date, Place		Summary of Events and Information	Remarks and references to Appendices
ST. RIQUIER.			
August 10. 1916.	6.30 am	Battn carried out attack in conjunction with 21st 22nd & 24th Battns on training ground.	
" 11.	6 am	Battn marched Blangy area – breakfast in field – practise in attack, etc.	
	5.30 pm	Capt fired a range etc tanks in pit.	
		Bn. Band playing	
" 12.	6am to 12 noon	Firing by Coys on ranges of 21st Divn Regt. 2 hrs. outpost instruction by Coys. Bombing under Battn B.O.	
" 13.	5.25 pm	Battn marched to training area turnmeries Battn B.O.	
		for night bayonet training 10.15 to 1.15 am.	
	5.3.30 am	Breakfast in field. Battalion in Bde. assault practice	
" 14.	6.15 am	Breakfast in field. Battn practise in attack.	
"	9 pm	Battn carried out night assault – area essential wood in practice of 12/8/16.	
" 15.			
" 16.	7am	Battn. training Reinforcements - 11 O.R. arrived.	
" 17.	6 am	Physical training. 8 am Battn parade for battn. training – digging, etc.	
	9 pm	Officers recon'd of Coys – marching on compass bearings.	

Army Form C. 2118.

WAR DIARY or INTELLIGENCE SUMMARY.

(Erase heading not required.)

Instructions regarding War Diaries and Intelligence Summaries are contained in F.S. Regs., Part II. and the Staff Manual respectively. Title pages will be prepared in manuscript.

Hour, Date, Place		Summary of Events and Information	Remarks and references to Appendices
ST. RIQUIER.			
18th August 1916.	4.45 am	Bn. Training attack practice	
	9 pm	Night Operations.	
19th 1916	10 am	Bn. Route march. Reinforcing draft of 101 O.R. arrived from Base	
20th 1916	8.30	Bn. Training. Coy Bombers throwing live grenades under Bombing Officer	
	5 pm	" paraded & marched to FRANCIERES (5 miles)	
FRANCIERES 1916	7.30 am	" " " " " VIGNACOURT (9)	
VIGNACOURT			
22nd	7 am	" " " " " VILLERS BOCAGE	
VILLERS BOCAGE			
23rd	9 am	" " " " " LAHOUSSOYE	
LAHOUSSOYE			
24th	6-6.30 am	Bayonet fighting. 7.30 am Bn parade. Coy. Training in close order drill	
	2.30 pm	extended, open attack. Bn. Drill	
25th	6.6.30 am	Bayonet fighting. 8 am Bn. paraded for digging. Specialist under Specialist Officers	
		Night operations	
26th	8.30 am	A & B Coy. on range; C & D Coy digging; Bombers & Lewis Gunners training	
	2.30 pm	Batt. Drill Ceremonial Drill	
27th	10 am	Church Parade. Inspection of billets by C.O. 2/Lt W. LEWIS reported for duty	
28th	6-6.30 am	Bayonet fighting. 8 am Digging & musketry	

WAR DIARY
or
INTELLIGENCE SUMMARY.
(Erase heading not required.)

Army Form C. 2118.

Hour, Date, Place	Summary of Events and Information	Remarks and references to Appendices
LAHOUSSOYE.		
29th August 1916. 6-6.30 am	Physical training. 8 am Digging & musketry. L.G. & Bombers training.	
8 pm	Bn. paraded for attack practice.	
30th 1916 8.30 am	C & D Coys. on range. A & B Coys. musketry, smoke helmet drill, extended order drill.	
9 am	Coy. Bombers under Bde B.O. at Bde Bombing Pit.	
Bn Parliament (see 31st)	Lectures by Coy. Cmdrs. on attack, gas, musketry &c.	
31st 1916 6.9.30	Musketry instruction under Coy. arrangements.	
8 am	C & D on range; A & B, musketry, smoke helmet drill	
2.30 pm	Bn. paraded, with band, for route march	

McKenzie Lt Col
comdg 1/22 Londoners

WAR DIARY or INTELLIGENCE SUMMARY

Army Form C. 2118.

1/23 London Regt.

1/23rd BATTN.
THE LONDON
REGIMENT

Hour, Date, Place	Summary of Events and Information	Remarks and references to Appendices
LAMOUSSOYE		
1st Sept. 1916. 7.45 a.m.	2 Officers & 150 men passed through gas School at PONT NOYELLES.	
6 a.m - 7 a.m.	Physical drill.	
8.30 "	Bn. training.	
2.30 - 4.30 p.m	Coys. musketry instruction. Specialist training under Specialist Officers	
2nd Septr 1916. 7.30 a.m.	Brigade attack practice	
3rd " 1916. 9.30 -	Church Parade. Draft of 37 other ranks arrived.	
4th " 1916. 6 -	Bayonet fighting.	
" 8.30	Bn. training - attack practice	
" 2.30 pm	Coy. " (musketry). Specialists under Specialist Officers.	
5th " 1916. 6 a.m.	Bayonet fighting & physical training	
" 8 "	Bn. (less "A Coy") paraded for extended order drill, musketry & smoke. Lewis drill.	
" 2 p.m.	A Coy training with 142 Trench Mortar Battery & Bde. Bombing Officers. All officers, W.O.s & N.C.O.s attended Trench Mortar demonstration.	
6th " 1916. 8.30 a.m.	Bn. Training (musketry on range).	
" 2.30-4.30 p.	Coys. under Coy Commanders for gas Helmet drill, musketry, kit inspection.	
7th - 6.30 a.m.	Bayonet fighting & physical training independently	
" 8.30	Bn. training. Specialist training under Specialist Officers	
" 2.30 p.m.	Lectures by Coy Commanders on modern attack, including Gas, Stoney points, Artillery barrage, Aeroplane contacts, Patrols & counter-attack.	

Army Form C. 2118.

WAR DIARY
or
INTELLIGENCE SUMMARY.
(Erase heading not required.)

Instructions regarding War Diaries and Intelligence Summaries are contained in F.S. Regs., Part II and the Staff Manual respectively. Title pages will be prepared in manuscript.

1/28rd BATT.N.
THE LONDON
REGIMENT.

Hour, Date, Place	Summary of Events and Information	Remarks and references to Appendices
LAHOUSSOYE		
8th September 1916.	Parades as yesterday.	
9th " 6.30am	Running drill.	
" 8.30 "	Battn. training.	
" 2.30 p	Lectures by Coy Commanders.	
10th " 8.15am	Bn. paraded and marched to ALBERT.	
ALBERT		
11th Sept. 1916 8.15am	Bn. marched to MAMETZ WOOD (in reserve).	
13 "	" moved to BAZENTIN-LE-PETIT. ('C' Coy. to HIGH WOOD)	
14th "	" " HIGH WOOD.	
15 "	Bn. placed at disposal of 140th Infy. Bde. and attacked at 9.25 am. (Bn had B Coy, but plus a Coy of 22nd Bn. Lon Regt.) Distance of advance, 1,500 yards on magnetic bearing of 29°. Left flank directed on COUGH DROP, right flank to pivot on COUGH DROP. The whole Bn. to consolidate on line along crest running N.E. unit patrols pushed into EAUCOURT L'ABBAYE. Right Coy. to gain touch with 6th Bn. Lon Regt. at junction of FLERS LINE and DROP ALLEY, left Coy. to endeavour to get into touch with 50th Division on PRUE TRENCH. The Right Coy. were to push out strong patrols to EAUCOURT L'ABBAYE and its left a strong patrol along the ridge towards 50th Division.	
	No preliminary reconnaissance of ground was made as there was not sufficient time.	

WAR DIARY
or
INTELLIGENCE SUMMARY

(Erase heading not required.)

Army Form C. 2118.

1/23RD BATTN.,
THE LONDON
REGIMENT.

Hour, Date, Place	Summary of Events and Information	Remarks and references to Appendices
(Contd) 16th September 1916.	At 8.55 a.m. the leading platoons deployed and moved forward on the crest in line, the other platoons following at fifty paces distance. The Battn. reached the crest in 4 waves, followed by Bombers, in fact order, without casualties. East of HIGH WOOD they were subjected to heavy barrage fire. At 10.25 a.m. reports came back that the attack was going well. Bn. was subjected to very heavy machine gun fire in reaching sunken road. After that, patrols were sent out encountering German posts and patrols and made prisoners among them an officer. Casualties very heavy, being brought in from neighbourhood of sunken road. At 2 am 17/9/16 the position was handed over to O.C. 6th Bn. London Regt. The attack proceeded in good order until they passed the firs ground around COUGH DROP, after that the attack was exposed to very heavy enfilade fire from both flanks and must also have suffered from our own artillery. The trenches were obliterated and the ridge is far from being a feature of the ground.	
17th September 1916.	The Commanding Officer handed over command of Bn. to Major HARGREAVES at 7 p.m. The remainder of the Bn. was pieces in support of 2/6 Bn London Regt, and with 3 Companies of the 24th Bn, were ordered to attack part of STARFISH	

WAR DIARY or INTELLIGENCE SUMMARY

Army Form C. 2118.

1/23RD BATT'N. THE LONDON REGIMENT.

Hour, Date, Place	Summary of Events and Information	Remarks and references to Appendices
18th September 1916.	Here in the early morning of 18th inst. The attack was continued and the STARFISH Line (final objective) was captured. During the advance from the N. corner of HIGH WOOD the enemy put out heavy barrage, and about 100 yds. from 1st objective the advance was held up foot & horse by very heavy machine gun fire from the left. The advance was reorganised and continued, & on reaching objective it was at once consolidated, commenced and carried on. About 10 a.m. a very strong bombing counter-attack was launched from a strong point on the left of the captured trench which drove the garrison out. A position was taken up about 100 yds. from where the bombing attack took place and 23rd & 24th Bns. were engaged the whole day (10 a.m. till dusk) in very heavy hand to hand bombing fighting. Official records of whose message, were wired by the Adjutant (Lieut. W. A. NEWTON) as soon as he saw the attack develop.	
	The Battalion was relieved about 10.30 pm by 22nd Bn. Inf. Regt. Casualties: 15-19/9/16 - 16 Officers & 565 other ranks.	
19th September 1916	Bn. marched to bivouac at BLACKWOOD, near ALBERT.	2/Lt. 29. THOMSON rejoined
20th " 1916	" " " MEAULTE COURT.	
22nd " 1916	Draft of 306 other ranks joined.	

Army Form C. 2118.

WAR DIARY
or
INTELLIGENCE SUMMARY

(Erase heading not required.)

Instructions regarding War Diaries and Intelligence Summaries are contained in F. S. Regs., Part II. and the Staff Manual respectively. Title pages will be prepared in manuscript.

Hour, Date, Place	Summary of Events and Information	Remarks and references to Appendices
MELLIN COURT.		
23rd September 1916. 8.30–	A + B Coys musketry instruction & close order drill. Bombers under Bombing Officer	
1 pm	C + D " " on range	
1–5	A + B " " "	
	C + D " musketry instruction + close order drill	
24th 9 am	Church Parade.	
10.30 "	Training of draft. L.G. instruction.	
25	Bn on range for musketry. 2/Lt G.C. TURNER rejoined	
	C. + D. Coys. attack practice	
26th 8.30 am	Attack practice	
27 8.30 "	Coys + Detachments training under own arrangements.	
11.30 "	Attack Practice	
28th 1.40 pm	Bn. paraded + marched to forward area in reserve (QUADRANGLE, near MAMETZ.	
29th " "	Draft of 56 other ranks arrived	
30" " "	2/Lt E. WARREN reported from Hospital.	
	Bn. moved to STARFISH Line, being placed at disposal of 141st Infantry Brigade.	

H.H. Kemble Lt Colonel,
Comdg. 1/23rd Bn. The London Regt.

123RD BATTN.
THE LONDON
REGIMENT.

WAR DIARY
or
INTELLIGENCE SUMMARY.
(Erase heading not required.)

Army Form C. 2118.

1/23 London Regt
Vol 20

559

Hour, Date, Place	Summary of Events and Information	Remarks and references to Appendices
1st Octr 1916.	Battalion in QUADRANGLE	
8.30 a.m	Moved to SWITCH LINE arriving at Noon. Battalion placed at disposal of 141st INF BDE at 5.30 P.M. Under orders of 141st INF BDE Battalion moved forward to PRUE TRENCH, one Company being detailed to carry bombs from HIGH WOOD. Headquarters to STARFISH. AT 9.30 P.M. further move into OB.I, and at 11 P.M. turning over recent to reinforce 141st INF BDE through EAUCOURT L'ABBAYE at dawn. Final orders received	
October 2nd 1916.	and detailed at 4.0 A.M, and after delay owing to congestion of trenches, advance was made from OB.I, in 4 attacking waves at 6.45 am. CAPT A.T. FERREN in Command of firing line. The attack was held up by heavy machine gun fire and CAPT. FERRON was ordered to reorganise in OB.I. Battalion Withdrew at dusk under orders of 141st INF BDE to PRUE TRENCH and later was ordered to move back to HIGH WOOD, and was placed under orders of 142nd INF BDE. Headquarters in BLACK WATCH TRENCH at 10 P.M. Casualties 5 KILLED, 83 WOUNDED, and 75 MISSING. At 6 P.M. MAJOR T.C. HARGREAVES took over Command of the Battalion. Officer Casualties - Wounded LT. R. BULGIN, 2Lts. R.G. THOMSON, H. SELTON, W.E. JONES, W.A. WEEDEN, J. HERRATT, E. M. PAYNE	
October 3rd 1916.	Battalion mustered in BLACK WATCH TRENCH by 5.0 A.M. while	
October 4th 1916.	day spent in reorganisation. Battalion supplied burying, fatigue and salvage parties	

WAR DIARY or INTELLIGENCE SUMMARY

Army Form C. 2118.

Hour, Date, Place	Summary of Events and Information	Remarks and references to Appendices
October 5th 1916.	Permanent Working Parties supplied for Light Railway and for Trench Mortar Battery.	H.J.N. Kennedy Lt Col 1/5/SS
October 6th 1916. October 7th 1916.	Battalion supplied burying, fatigue and salvage parties. Parts of 60 other ranks placed at disposal of Staff Captain 142nd Inf Bde. Reconnaissance of EAUCOURT L'ABBAYE carried out by Officers.	
October 8th 1916 – 5.0 P.M.	Battalion moved forward to Brigade Reserve. Headquarters at STARFISH. Battalion, less permanent working party, in FLERS SWITCH and PRUE TRENCH. At 11 P.M. one Company was ordered to reinforce 21st Manchester Regt in front of EAUCOURT L'ABBAYE, and the party of 60 other ranks under 2/Lt. C.J. CREED, which had been left at HIGH WOOD at disposal of Staff Capt, was ordered to take the place of reserve troops in FLERS SWITCH. At 12 midnight a second party, consisting of the Garrison Prue Trench, moved up to reinforce 21st Manchester Regt. These reinforcements were carried out under the command of Capt. R.H. TOLERTON, who then placed himself under the command of O/C 21st Manchester Regt.	
October 9th 1916. 5 A.M.	Capt. R.H. TOLERTON reported that he had relieved 21st Manchester Regt. At the same time 2 parts of 22 Manchester troops were sent from STARFISH to assist in removing 21st Manchester wounded. Disposition of Capt. TOLERTON'S troops :- Details of A Coy in Strong Point	

560

ns/C. 2118/10.

WAR DIARY
or
INTELLIGENCE SUMMARY.
(Erase heading not required.)

Army Form C. 2118.

561

H. H. Nixon Lt Col
1/23 London

H. H.

Hour, Date, Place	Summary of Events and Information	Remarks and references to Appendices
October 10th 1916.	under LT. D.J. WARDLEY; remainder in front line and QUARRY. At 6.30 PM Battalion relieved by a SOUTH AFRICAN Battalion & the 9th Division and moved back to the QUADRANGLE.	
October 11th 1916.	Lt. Col. H.H. KEMBLE, M.C. proceed on leave to U.K. Battalion moved from QUADRANGLE to LAVEVILLE arriving at 5.30 P.M. Battalion billeted in close billets.	
October 12th 1916.	Interior economy. Morning, refitting and fatigue parties. LTS. C.A.C. ROWLEY, P.R. HONEYBALL and 2/LTS. W.A. SOLVEN, H.S. ELTON, C.J. CREED and W.LE WIS returned from hospital. 2/LT. W.V. SCULTHORPE from Divisional School. CAPTAIN	
October 13th 1916.	R.S.M. GRINDEL, 2/LT. J.D.L. REID joined from England Battalion inspected by CORPS COMMANDER in morning. Battle at BAISIEUX 1-4 P.M. Rest of day, interior economy. CAPT. A.T. FERRON on short leave to England.	
October 14th 1916.	Battalion moved to PONT REMY. C and D Companies under CAPT. R.H. TOLERTON marched to ALBERT and entrained at 11 A.M., arriving LONGPRE 5 A.M. 15/10/16, and reaching PONT REMY at 9.30 A.M. A and B Coys and H.Q. Details under LT. C.A.C. ROWLEY entrained at ALBERT at 2 P.M., detrained at LONGPRE at 8.30 A.M. and arrived at PONT REMY at 1.30 P.M. Draft of 185 other ranks (transferred from CITY OF LONDON YEOMANRY) joined Battalion at entraining point. LT. H.B.N. NIXON joined from England.	

Army Form C. 2118.

WAR DIARY
or
INTELLIGENCE SUMMARY.
(Erase heading not required.)

1/23 London Regt   Oct 1916

Instructions regarding War Diaries and Intelligence Summaries are contained in F.S. Regs., Part II. and the Staff Manual respectively. Title pages will be prepared in manuscript.

Hour, Date, Place	Summary of Events and Information	Remarks and references to Appendices
October 15th 1916.	Billets in close billets at PONT REMY	
October 16th 1916.	Battalion entrained at PONT REMY for GOODERSWAARDE, arriving at 9 P.M. and marched to PATRICIA LINES, POPERINGHE, arriving at 3.0 A.M. 17/10/16.	
October 17th 1916.	Interior economy	
October 18th 1916.	Draft of 102 other ranks arrived from England. Billets at Brandwick Billets, POPERINGHE.	H.M. Kemmels D.V.S. 28 London
October 19th 1916.	Battn in morning. Battalion moved to BRANDHOEK and returned to YPRES district and relieved 24th AUSTRALIAN BATTN at RAILWAY DUGOUTS. Disposition of Companies :- A+B Companies RAILWAY DUGOUTS, C Coy at S.P.9, D Coy at BATTERIES FARM	
October 20th - 24th 1916.	Companies acted as working and carrying parties at shipyard. 2/Lts. G. GORDON and F.H. PAGE joined from England 21/10/16.	
October 24th/25th 1916.	Battalion relieved 24th London Regt in HILL 60 Sector. Disposition of Companies :- D left, A centre, C right, B in close support. Draft of 49 other ranks arrived from England. 2/Lt. H.S. EWEN arrived from England. At 2 A.M. 29th Oct. 2nd CANADIAN TUNNELLING COY blew up a camouflet No pullies	
October 28th 1916.	CAPT. J. ROOKE-COWELL, 2/LTS. K.I. NEWELL, D.C. HUGHES, G.K.G. BETTANY, J.M. BAILEY (from City of London Yeomanry) joined from England.	562
October 29th 1916.	Battalion relieved by 2nd Bn. Border Regt and moved to HALIFAX CAMP, arriving at 12 midnight.	

Army Form C. 2118.

WAR DIARY
or
INTELLIGENCE SUMMARY.
(Erase heading not required.)

Instructions regarding War Diaries and Intelligence Summaries are contained in F.S. Regs., Part II. and the Staff Manual respectively. Title pages will be prepared in manuscript.

Hour, Date, Place	Summary of Events and Information	Remarks and references to Appendices
October 30th 1916	CAPT. C. McQ. JOHNSTON, CAPT. A.C.TREMBATH, 2/LTS. A.T.G.L.NIBBS, and F.C.FRYE joined from England. Posted to Divisional Battn. Interim economy.	
October 31st 1916.	All Officers paraded at M.O's hut for instruction in use of new Box Gas Respirator. 50 men detailed for Permanent Working Party at DECAUVILLE railway. Batch (at Divisional Battn. Interim economy.	

H.H. Kemble Lt. Col.
Commdg 1/23rd Bn. The London Regt.

1/23rd Batt'n London Regt
Vol 21

WAR DIARY
or
INTELLIGENCE SUMMARY.
(Erase heading not required.)

Army Form C. 2118.

Instructions regarding War Diaries and Intelligence Summaries are contained in F.S. Regs., Part II and the Staff Manual respectively. Title pages will be prepared in manuscript.

Hour, Date, Place	Summary of Events and Information	Remarks and references to Appendices
HALIFAX CAMP		
1st November 1916	Parades for instruction in new box respirator. A & B Coys pass through Gas at GAS HUT – 2 to 5 p.m.	
2nd " "	C – D " " " " " 10 a.m. – 1 "	
3rd " "	" " " " " " 10 a.m. – 1 "	
4th " "	Bn. bathed at HALIFAX baths. 8 – 12 noon	
"	moved into support on HILL 60 Sector. H.Q., C & D Coys. on BELGIAN CHATEAU. "A" Coy in RAILWAY DUGOUTS, "B" Coy LARCH WOOD. Capt G.A. BRETT rejoined from England.	
BELGIAN CHATEAU		
5th Nov. 1916. 10 a.m.	Church Parade.	
6th " "	Rifle Section reconnoitred by Coy Commanders.	
7th " "		
8th " "	Bn. relieved by 7th Bn. and marched to DOMINION LINES.	
DOMINION LINES		
9th Nov 1916.	Kit re inspection & cleaning up	
10th "	Commanding Officer's Inspection, by Companies and Section.	
11" 8.30 – 9.30 a.m.	Squad drill. 9.30 – 10.15 Physical drill. 10.30 – 11.30 Company drill. 11.30 – 12.30 Ceremonial parade in 2.30 – 4. {A & C Coys route march. Specialists under own Officers. {B & D Coy – wiring practice.	
12" 1916 10 a.m.	Bde Church Parade. Medal ribbons presented to 7 N.C.O's & men by Gnl. Dgman.	
" 11 a.m.	Batt'n Church Parade under Adjutant	
13" " 1916 8.30 – 9.30	Squad drill. 9.30 – 10.15. Physical Training. Bayonet fighting. 10.35 – 11. Gas Drill 11 – 12.30 A & D Coy route march. B Coy elementary musketry. 2.30 – 4 p.m. A Coy wiring & digging. B & C Coy route march. D Coy wiring & digging.	

1/23 Bn London Regt
Army Form C. 2118.

WAR DIARY
or
INTELLIGENCE SUMMARY.
(Erase heading not required.)

Instructions regarding War Diaries and Intelligence Summaries are contained in F.S. Regs., Part II and the Staff Manual respectively. Title pages will be prepared in manuscript.

Hour, Date, Place	Summary of Events and Information	Remarks and references to Appendices
13th Nov 1916 (contd) 9-D-9.30 am	Camp inspected by Lt. Gen. Sir T. Morland, Cmdg. X Corps. Platoon drill. 9.30-10.15. Bayonet fighting. 10.30-1. Ceremonial, guards &c	
14th "	11-12.30. C Coy wiring & digging. 11-12. A & D Coys elementary musketry. 12-12.30. A&D. Gas Helmet drill in F.M.O.	
" Afternoon	"C" Coy on range. 2.30-4 pm. A&D. route march. 5.30-7. B Coy wiring. B Coy bathed at HOPOUTRE Siding. 10.30-12.30 pm. Camp inspected by Major Gen. Cavanagh, Cmdg 47th Division.	
15th " 8.30-12.30 am	A & C Coys at Baths, HOPOUTRE Siding. Physical training, musketry instruction & extended Order Drill.	
" 3 pm	Inspected by R.E. in trench construction by explosives.	
16th " 8.30-11.30 am and 2.30-3.30 pm.	Training as previous day	
17th " 8.30-11.30 am and 2.30-4 pm.	D Coy, S.B. + details bathed at HOPOUTRE. Training as on 16th. Coy Route marches	
18th " 12 noon	"C" Coy, Bombers & H.Q. details moved to SWAN CHATEAU (BLUFF Sector) A & B in "the BLUFF". D in Camp	
" 3 pm.	A, B, & D Coys move into support. Points by A and B, relieving 20th Bn Lon Regt.	
25th " 6 pm	"B" Coy relieved left Coy of 24th Bn Lon Regt. in front line	
26th " to 3	"C" " " " " " in TUNNELS.	
27th "	Nothing of special interest.	

(73969) W4141-163. 400,000. 9/14. H.&J.Ltd. Forms/C. 2118/10.

1/23rd Lon Regt.

Army Form C. 2118.

WAR DIARY
or
INTELLIGENCE SUMMARY.
(Erase heading not required.)

Hour, Date, Place		Summary of Events and Information	Remarks and references to Appendices
29th Nov. 1916	6 pm	Bn HQ now centre section of "Canal Sector" establishing H.Q at WOODCOTE HOUSE. Bombers & 2 platoon D Coy at WOODCOTE. 2 platoon in S.P. 7 + 8. A.B.C. Coys in line. A CENTRE B. RIGHT C LEFT	
30th Nov 1916	—	In trenches.	

H H Kemble
Lt. Col.
Comdg 1/23 Bn The Lon Regt.

Army Form C. 2118.

23rd Bn. The London Regt.

WAR DIARY
or
INTELLIGENCE SUMMARY

(Erase heading not required.)

Vol 22

1/23rd BATTN.
THE LONDON
REGIMENT.

Place	Date	Hour	Summary of Events and Information	Remarks and references to Appendices
CANAL SUB-SECTOR YPRES	1/12/16	—	Bn in trenches	
	2/12/16		D Coy relieved "B" in trenches Right Firing Line, "B" Coy moving 2 platoons to WOODCOTE FARM, 2 platoons in Strong Points 4 and 8.	
			Casualties: 1 OR Killed, 3 OR Wounded.	
	4/12/16		1 OR Killed, 2 OR wounded	
	6/12/16		3 OR Wounded	
	8/12/16	11 pm	Bn. relieved by 6th Bn London Regt.	
DOMINION	9/12/16	2 am	" arrived at DOMINION CAMP, relieving 1st Bn London Regt.	
	10/12/16	10 am	Camp inspected by Brig. Gen F.G. LEWIS, Cmdg. 142 Inf Bde.	
		16.30	Special Church Parade. 11 N.C.Os presented with M.M. ribbons by G.O.C. 47th Div.	
	11/12/16		Bn. Church Parade	
		8.30–11.30 am	Bathing at HOPOUTRE Siding. C.O. inspected Camp.	
	12/12/16		Pioneer Platoon of all Coys cleaning drains and Camp generally. Camp inspected by Major General Sir F. Gorringe, Cmdg. 47th Division. Coy Training.	
	13/12/16		3 Officers sent to Refilling Point, RENINGHELST for instruction.	
	13/12/16		36 O.R. sent to join Heavy Branch, M.G.C. (TANKS). Coy training.	
	14/12/16		Coy training. Brig. Gen. LEWIS inspected Camp. 1 Officer + 50 OR per Coy. attended demonstration in WIRING to by 1/4th London Field Coy. R.E. C.O. inspected Camp. prior to inspection by G.O.C. 47th Division. Coy Specialist training. Lewis Gun Section on range at DICKEBUSCH.	
	15/12/16	8.30 am		
		10.30–12 noon	Bathing at HOPOUTRE Siding. 2.30–3.30 pm. Bathing at HALIFAX.	

WAR DIARY
or
INTELLIGENCE SUMMARY

(Erase heading not required.)

Army Form C. 2118.

Place	Date	Hour	Summary of Events and Information	Remarks and references to Appendices
DOMINION	16/12/16		Coy and Specialist training. Sniper section on DICKEBUSCH range	
	17/12/16	10.30 am	Church Parade	
		1/30	C.O. inspected Camp.	
	18/12/16	12 noon	Orders received postponing relief of 18th Bn Lan Regt and Bn ordered to be ready to move instantly	
		2 pm	"Stand down" received.	
	19/12/16	3.45 pm	Bn paraded and marched to HILL 60 Sub-Sector, relieving 18th Bn Lan Regt D left, C centre, B right front line, A Coy in Reserve at RAILWAY DUGOUTS; H.Q. at LARCH WOOD. 1 O.R. Killed, 4 O.R. Wounded.	
	21/12/16		Capt A.C. TREMBATH (3/5 East Surrey Regt attd) and 3 O.R. KILLED.	
	22/12/16		2/Lt K.L. NEWELL & T.E. WEBSTER wounded (at duty); 12 O.R. Wounded.	
	24/12/16		Bn relieved by 24th Bn Lan Regt. H.Q. & 2 platoons D Coy to RAILWAY DUGOUTS; 2 platoons D Coy to FOSSE WAY; "A" Coy at BATTERSEA FARM; B + C Coy at CHATEAU BELGE.	
	27/12/16		2/Lts H.S. ELTON and J.M. BAILEY to Heavy Branch, M.G.C. (TANKS)	
	30/12/16		"C" Coy to BATTERSEA FARM, relieving "A" Coy, who went to CHATEAU BELGE.	

H.H. Kemble Lt. Colonel
Cmdg 1/23rd Bn The London Regt T.F.

Army Form C. 2118.

WAR DIARY
or
INTELLIGENCE SUMMARY
(Erase heading not required.)

1/2's London Regt

Vol 23

Place	Date	Hour	Summary of Events and Information	Remarks and references to Appendices
Hill Sd Sub.Sector YPRES.	1/1/17		1 O.R. wounded. Lt. Col H.H. KEMBLE, M.C., awarded D.S.O. (London Gazette)	
	4/1/17		1 " Killed	
	5/1/17		1 " Wounded	
	6/1/17		8 " Wounded. 2/Lt. W.R. WARNER (6o "Div. Cyclist) joined from Base.	
	7/1/17		Lt. Col. Kemble D.S.O, M.C. to 2nd Army School	
	8/1/17		1 O.R. Killed. Bn. relieved by 15th Bn. Lon. Regt. and marched to DOMINION Camp.	
DOMINION	9/1/17		Intense Economy.	
	10/1/17	9.30 am – 1.30 pm	Physical Training. 7.45 Coy. + Specialist Training.	
		7.45	3 N.C.O.s awarded MILITARY MEDAL for work during last tour.	
	11/1/17	8.30 a 12.30 p	Bn. baths at HOPOUTRE Siding, POPERINGHE. Draft of 50 O.R. from Base.	
	12/1/17	12.30 p	100 O.R. attended Bde Bomb School, HALIFAX, for bomb throwing practice.	
		8.30 a	Regular Lewis Gun Teams on DICKEBUSCH range under 2/Lt. T.E. WEBSTER. Coy. + Specialist Training	
	13/1/17		Coy. and Specialist Training.	
	14/1/17	10.30 am	all Officers, 100 O.R. and Drums attended Bde Church Service. Lt. Col. H.H. KEMBLE resumed command of the Bn.	
		12 noon	C.O. inspected Camp.	
			Coy. and Specialist Training	
	15/1/17		– do – 9 am – 12 noon. L.G. Teams at DICKEBUSCH Range under 2/Lt. IMISON	
			12 – 2 pm SNIPER Section " " " Lt. LATHAM.	
	16/1/17		2/Lt A. TUGWELL and H.W. FIETH joined from Base. Capt. G.E. PALMER from England	
		4 pm	Battn. moved to DICKEBUSCH Camp South.	

WAR DIARY or INTELLIGENCE SUMMARY

Army Form C. 2118.

Place	Date	Hour	Summary of Events and Information	Remarks and references to Appendices
DICKEBUSCH HUTS	17/1/17	9 am / 4 pm	Coy and Specialist Training	
	18/1/17	9 am	Lectures by Coy Commanders. Lt Col H.H. KEMBLE to England for 1 month's leave. 2/Lt REG BRIDGE from Base.	
	19/1/17	9.15 a	Coy Specialist Training, including 1 hr physical training. "A" Coy route march.	
	20/1/17	"	-do- "B" -do-	
	21/1/17	6 pm	"C" Coy Xmas Dinner. Major C.F.H. GREENWOOD, 1/23rd London Regt, assumed Command of Bn. 2/Lt G. FRANKLIN joined from Base.	
	22/1/17	9 am / 5 pm	Coy & Specialist training. "C" Coy route march. Working Party of 2 Officers and 100 o.r. "A" Coy. Draft of 25 o.r. from Base. "D" Coy Xmas Dinner.	
	23/1/17	"	Coy & Specialist training. D Coy route march. "A" Coy Xmas Dinner.	
	24/1/17	9 am	-do- (a) Reconnaissance of new sector by 1 Guide per platoon & specialist section. "G.H.Q. 2nd line" -do- 10 Officers via N.C.Os per Coy, I.O, 2 runners, 2 signallers.	
	25/1/17	9 am	-do- -do- -do- "front line in BLUFF Sub-Sector by Adjt. 1 Officer per Coy & Bombing Officer.	
	26/1/17	9 am	-do- -do- -do-	
	27/1/17		Bn. relieved 24th Bn. Lon. Regt. in BLUFF Sub-Sector. B Coy left, "A" Coy centre, "C" Coy right (Firing line) "D" Coy; Bombers and Bn. H.Q in BLUFF TUNNELS.	
Right section of CANAL sub-sector	28/1/17	-	2/Lt G.W. CRISP joined from England.	
"	29/1/17		In trenches as above.	
"	30/1/17			
BLUFF SECTOR	31/1/17			

Comdg 1/23 Bn. The London Regt.

C.F.H. Greenwood
Major
Regt

WAR DIARY or INTELLIGENCE SUMMARY

Army Form C. 2118.

1/23rd Batt. London Regt.

February 1917.

Place	Date	Hour	Summary of Events and Information	Remarks and references to Appendices
BLUFF Sector YPRES.	1/2/17 to 3/2/17		Bn. in Trenches. Nothing of any importance. 2/Lt. F.C. FRYE to command D Coy, vice Capt. ENTWISLE. Bn. relieved by 4th Bn. LON REGT 3/2/17 and marched to DOMINION Camp.	
	4/2/17		Interior Economy, cleaning up, &c.	
DOMINION.	5/2/17		Training under Coy arrangements. Raiding Party of 2 Officers + 50 O.R. trained.	
	6/2/17	11 am & 4 pm	Bn. bathed at HOPOUTRE Siding.	
	7/2/17		Coy. Specialist training.	
			-do- 40 O.R. on Bde Bomb Course, VANCOUVER.	
	8/2/17	8.30 am 9.30	Bathing at HOPOUTRE. Coy training. Capt. F. ENTWISLE to Hospital. Capt. R.H. TOLERTON 2nd-in-Command. 2/Lt. [MILSON?] to command 'C' Coy, vice Capt. TOLERTON.	
	9/2/17	10 am 8 am	Contact Patrol Aeroplane Practice carried out under Capt. G.A. BRETT. Coy.re Training. Range at DICKEBUSCH used by Lewis Gunners.	
	10/2/17		Coy training. Bn. Bombing Platoon broken up and men distributed amongst Companies.	
	11/2/17	4 pm	Bn. relieved 17th Bn. LON. REGT. in HILL 60 Sub-Sector, Left Section. H.Q. B and C Coys at RAILWAY DUGOUTS, A and C Coys. at BELGIAN CHATEAU. Working party of 58 O.R. attached to Australian Tunnelling Co.	
	12/2/17		3 platoons "D" Coy. to BATTERSEA FARM. 2/Lt's } ROOKE - COWELL Casualties - 1 O.R. Wounded (1 at duty)	
	13/2/17 14/2/17 15/2/17	-	1 " " Bn. moved into Front Line - C right, A centre, B left, D at Railway 2 " " " Dugouts (1 platoon FOSSE WAY).	
	17/2/17			

Army Form C. 2118.

WAR DIARY
or
INTELLIGENCE SUMMARY
(Erase heading not required.)

Instructions regarding War Diaries and Intelligence Summaries are contained in F. S. Regs., Part II. and the Staff Manual respectively. Title Pages will be prepared in manuscript.

Place	Date	Hour	Summary of Events and Information	Remarks and references to Appendices
HILL 60	17/2/17		P.W.P. attd Australian Tunnelling Co. invalided to B. 123 O.R. and 1 Officer (2/Lt H.W. FIETH)	
	19/2/17		Casualties: 1 OR wounded	
			" 1 " Killed, 4 OR Wounded	
	20/2/17		6th Bn LON REGT carried out raid in BLUFF SECTOR. Feind attack made on our front, including 1 mine and 1 camouflet 41mm. 1 Officer + 119 OR taken by 6th LON REGT, also 4 machine guns.	
	21/2/17		Casualties: 1 OR Killed + 1 OR Wounded	
	22/2/17		" 1 " Wounded	
	25/2/17		Lt Col. H.A. KEMBLE, D.S.O., M.C. rejoined from England, 2/Lt F.R. HONEYBALL from Base.	
	26/2/17		Casualties: 1 OR. Killed, 2 OR. Wounded	
	27/2/17		" 1 " " 4 " " Bn. relieved by 6th Bn LON REGT. and marched to	
	28/2/17		DOMINION. Major CFH GREENWOOD rejoined 22nd Bn Lon Regt.	
			Interior economy, cleaning up, etc.	

    1/23rd BATTN.
    THE LONDON
    REGIMENT.
    2-3-17

H H Kemble Lieut Colonel,
Commanding 1/23rd Bn. The London Regiment.

Army Form C. 2118.

1/23rd BATTN.
THE LONDON
REGIMENT.

No. ....
Date ....

WAR DIARY
or
INTELLIGENCE SUMMARY.

(Erase heading not required.)

MARCH, 1917.

Instructions regarding War Diaries and Intelligence Summaries are contained in F. S. Regs., Part II. and the Staff Manual respectively. Title pages will be prepared in manuscript.

Place	Date	Hour	Summary of Events and Information	Remarks and references to Appendices
DOMINION CAMP	1/3/17	am 7.30 – 1.30 –	Physical Training. Coy Drill, Route march. Specialist training. 8.30 A.M.) Battn. bathed at 5 pm SHOPOUTRE, POPERINGHE.	
— " —	2/3/17	" " "	— " — Riding party trained under 2/Lt G.K.F. BETTANY and G. FORDON	
— " —	3/3/17	9.30–12.30 P.M.	Range at DICKEBUSCH allotted to A + B Coy L.Gs. 2-5 pm to C + D. Coy L.G.s Coy Training. 80 Rifle Bombers at Bde Bomb School, HALIFAX	
— " —	4/3/17	10 A.M.	Parade Service at SCOTTISH LINES. C.O. inspected camp.	
— " —	5/3/17	9 –	C.O. inspected each Coy separately. Manual Coy Training. 2/Lts C.R. MARSHALL & A.W. DURRANT from Base	
— " —	6/3/17	9 A.M. 10.30 "	"C" Coy + Signallers at Divl. Gas School, BUSSEBOOM. Training against Gas Shells.}Manual Coy & Training "D" — Ditto	
— " —	7/3/17		Camp inspected by Major-Gen. G.F. GORRINGE.	
— " —	8/3/17	9 A.M. 3 PM	A Coy at Divl. Gas School. 10.30 A.M. "B" Coy. Coy Training till 11 P.M. Bn. moved into Bde. Reserve in CANAL Reserve Camp, relieving 20"B" The London Regt.	
DICKEBUSCH	9/3/17	9AM-12 noon	Training under Coy +c arrangements. C.O inspected Camp. A Coy bathed at HALIFAX (A.M. 6.30)	
— " —	9/3/17		— " — 8.30–11 A.M. 500 R. each of Band C Coy bathed at HALIFAX.	
— " —	10/3/17	3.0 pm	Working Party of 18 officers + 30 O.R. ("C" Coy) constructing range at VANCOUVER Camp, daily 9-12.30. 50 O.R. D Coy bathed at HALIFAX. Training as usual.	
— " —	11/3/17	9 am	Holy Communion. 6 Pln. Voluntary Service. Minor Training 9.45-11.15 A.M.	

T2134. Wt. W708–776. 500000. 4/15. Sir J. C. & S.

Army Form C. 2118.

WAR DIARY
INTELLIGENCE SUMMARY
(Erase heading not required.)

1/28RD
THE LONDON
REGIMENT.

Instructions regarding War Diaries and Intelligence Summaries are contained in F. S. Regs., Part II. and the Staff Manual respectively. Title pages will be prepared in manuscript.

Place	Date	Hour	Summary of Events and Information	Remarks and references to Appendices
DICKEBUSCH	12/7/17	9 A.M.	12 noon. Coy. & Training. 0. F.C. FRYE to Hospital. 3 P.M. Lecture by M.O. to all Officers + N.C.O's	
	13/3/17		50 O.R. (Specialists) batted at HALIFAX. Coy. Commanders reconnitred line	
			9.15 - 9.45.	
	14/3/17		Bn. moved into Right Sector, CANAL Sub Sector, YPRES, relieving 24th Bn London Regt. C Coy left. "D" Coy right firing line, A Coy support, B Coy reserve H.Q. in TUNNELS. Capt. FENTWISLE from H.Q.	
CANAL Sub Sector	19/3/17		A Coy relieved "C" Coy. "B" Coy. relieved D Coy. in CRATERS.	
	21/3/17		Bn. relieved by 7th Bn London Regt. and marched to DOMINION CAMP	
	22/3/17		Interior economy, cleaning up, &c. L.F.R. HONEYBALL to England for transfer to Indian Army.	
DOMINION	23/3/17	9 a.m.	Bn. paraded and marched to STEENVOORDE – Being marching past G.O.C. 2nd Army en route.	
STEENVOORDE	24/3/17	A.M.(11)	" ARNÉKE. 2/Lts W.E. PHILLIPS and L.J. KENT-JONES from Base. 23/7	
ARNÉKE	25/3/17	A.M. 9.30	" HOULLE – dinners on march, arriving at 5 p.m. Capt H.B.N. NIXON and 2/Lt. H.STONE from A/Lt 24/3, Capt. R.S.M. GRINDEL 25/7.	
HOULLE	26/3/17	9 P.M.	Battalion Drill in Training Area	
	27/3/17	9.45	C.O's Parade. 6.45 am Roll call + 10 minutes running.	
	28/3/17	6.45	Roll call + 10 mins running. 9AM – 1 P.M. – Platoon Training near Coy. billets.	241

Army Form C. 2118.

WAR DIARY
INTELLIGENCE SUMMARY.

(Erase heading not required.)

Instructions regarding War Diaries and Intelligence Summaries are contained in F. S. Regs., Part II. and the Staff Manual respectively. Title pages will be prepared in manuscript.

1/23RD BATT.
THE LONDON
REGIMENT.

No. ....
Date ....

Place	Date	Hour	Summary of Events and Information	Remarks and references to Appendices
HOULLE	29/3/17	6.45AM	Roll call & 10 minutes running. 9AM-1PM. Outdoor Coy Training. D and C Coys each 2 hours on Range for musketry, each 1 hr for L.G. practice. B and A Coys 2 hours in an Assault Course.	
		P.M. 2-4.30	Signals, Runners and "B" Coy bathed at HOULLE Baths. Major T.C. HARGREAVES, D.S.O. from England, is	
		6 p.m.	Lecture to Officers and N.C.O.s by 4th J.D.L. REID on "Platoon in the attack". [He second in command]	
—	30/3/17	6.45AM	10 minutes running. 9AM-1PM. Coy Training. A and B Coys on Range 2 hours each, 1 hr each for L.G. practice. C and D Coys each 2 hours on Assault Course.	
		6 p.m.	Lecture by Medical Officer to Officers and N.C.O.s — "Care of feet on the march". Capt C.A.C. ROWLEY from Hospital.	
—	31/3/17	6.45AM	10 minutes running. 9AM - 1PM. Coy Training. Inter Platoon Competition in Bombing attack (1 Platoon per Coy) and in Bayonet Fighting.	
		3 pm	Batt. Training Competition (1 Platoon per Coy.)	

2nd April 1917

H.M.Kemble Lieut Colonel,
Comdg. 1/23rd Battn. The London Regiment.

Army Form C. 2118.

WAR DIARY

INTELLIGENCE SUMMARY

1/23rd Bn. The London Regt.

(*Erase heading not required.*)

Vol 26

Instructions regarding War Diaries and Intelligence Summaries are contained in F. S. Regs., Part II. and the Staff Manual respectively. Title Pages will be prepared in manuscript.

Place	Date	Hour	Summary of Events and Information	Remarks and references to Appendices
	April 1917.			
HOUlle P.-de-C.	1	11.30 A	Parade Service	
	2	9.30 A	C Coy on Range; 10.45, B Coy; 2.30 P.M., A Coy; 3.45 P.M, D Coy. Platoon drill Competition (1. Turn-out, 2. Command, 3. Close 'extended order drill) won by No 5 (2)/Lt Mc EWEN	
		8.45 A.	Bombing Attack practice under 2/Lt J.D.L REID Platoon Bayonet fighting comp by No 6 (2/Lt P.M.MITCHELL); Bombing by No 14 (2/Lt H.W FIETH). Capt. C.A.C. ROWLEY assumed command of "A" Coy vice Capt. G.A BRETT.	
-//-	3	8.30 AM	Bombing Attack practice (as 2nd).	
		9.30 -	Bn. and Coy. training.	
-//-	4	8.30 AM	Bombing Attack practice. 9.30. Bn. and Coy. Training.	
-//-	5	9.30 "	Bn. and Coy. Training.	
-//-	6	9.30 "	Bn. Attack Practice.	
-//-	7	9.30 "	Bn. and Coy. Training.	
		2 pm	& D Coy futdes at HOULLE Baths. 3 pm. "C" Coy 4 P.M. "A" Coy	
-//-	8	9.15 AM	Bn. paraded and marched to ARNEKE, arriving at 4 p.m.	
ARNEKE	9	7.40 AM	" " ", STEENVOORDE area, arriving at noon.	
STEENVOORDE	10		Commanding Officer inspected Coys. and billets. 4 Officers & 105 O.R. A Coy. as Permanent Working Party, marched to VANCOUVER Camp under Capt. G.A BRETT.	

WAR DIARY or INTELLIGENCE SUMMARY

Army Form C. 2118.

1/23rd Bn. The London Regt.

Place	Date	Hour	Summary of Events and Information	Remarks and references to Appendices
	April, 1917			
STEENVOORDE	11	8.30 AM	Bn. marched to HALIFAX Camp, arriving at 1 P.M. 2/Lt. C.H. NEEDEN joined for duty.	
HALIFAX	12		Coy. inspections and refitting	
	13	9 AM - 12.30 PM	"B" Coy inoculated. A Coy refitting. C and D Coy. Specialist Training. Capt. G.C. PHILLIPS rejoined from England. 2/Lt. (?) D. HYAMS sick to Hospital.	
			500 O.R. employed on sanitary work under M.O.	
	14	9 am - 12.30 pm	Specialist Training.	
	15	8 AM	Holy Communion. 11.30 A.M. - Church Service in CANTEEN.	
	16	9 AM - 12.30 PM	Coy Training. "D" Coy inoculated. Commanding Officer inspected Camp.	
		1 P.M.	A and B Coy Lewis Gun Teams on range (2 hours each).	
	17	9 AM 12.30 ?	Coy Training. 2/Lt. W.R. WARNER sick to Hpt.	
	18	--	400 men trained at HALIFAX	
	19	--	180 men trained at HALIFAX. Major A.T. FERRON, M.C. attd 1/4 Bn London Regt.	
			Bn. relieved 24th Bn London Regt. in RIGHT Section, CANAL Sub-Sectn, YPRES. D Coy left, B Coy right, Firing line, C Coy support, A Coy Res (3 platoons) Reserve.	
CANAL Sub-Sectn YPRES	22		2 O.R. Wounded	
	24	3.30 AM	Our trenches I.34.1, 2 and 3 (28NW), North of BLUFF, were unsuccessfully attacked by an enemy raiding party about 50 strong. The trench is some 300 yds. in length was garrisoned by 1 platoon with 4 Lewis guns by night or 2 L.G. by day. Alarm light signals	

WAR DIARY or INTELLIGENCE SUMMARY

Army Form C. 2118.

1/23rd / 13th The London Regt.

Place	Date	Hour	Summary of Events and Information	Remarks and references to Appendices
	April 19 24 (contd)		were fired from enemy lines during the night and our sentries were alert. At 3.30 P.M. the enemy who had detected leaving their trench. Immediately afterwards the enemy put up an intense barrage with field guns and a few Howitz and Minenwerfers on our support and reserve lines. Our garrison opened fire at once on advancing enemy. Our S.O.S failed; the very light signals misfired and S.O.S wire was broken in 5 places. Information was sent to Bn. H.Q. by runner. The enemy reached bombing distance, 5 of them mounting our trench. The garrison suffered 13 casualties, principally from bombs. They kept up a steady fire and drove the enemy back to their trench. As the enemy reached their trench, our artillery opened fire. There were several wounded among the enemy, and one was left lying dead in NO MAN'S LAND. 2/Lt. W. BLIGHT, Artists Rifles (attd), 703221 4/Cpl. S.F. LOADER and 703880 4/Cpl. N.R. SCUDAMORE especially distinguished themselves. Valuable assistance was rendered by the right posts of the 22nd Bn. London Regt. on our left, who supported us with enfilade fire. "C" Coy. relieved "B" Coy. who moved to support.	
	25	4.30 AM	The 22nd Bn. on our left, were attacked by a raiding party. The raid was the same strength + organised on the same lines as on the previous night. Our left post rendered vigorous assistance. The enemy was driven off, leaving 2 or 3 dead. 59044 Pte E GILBERT 1/28th Bn London Regt. (attd.) KILLED. 2 O.R. wounded.	
	26		2 Platoons "B" Coy + "A" Coy relieved "D" Coy on left Front; 2 Platoons D to support, 2 to reserve. Capt. R.S.M. GRINDEL to Hospital (sick).	
	28	9.30 PM	Bn. (less B Coy) relieved by 24th Bn London Regt and marched to OTTAWA Camp.	

Army Form C. 2118.

WAR DIARY

INTELLIGENCE SUMMARY

(Erase heading not required.)

Instructions regarding War Diaries and Intelligence Summaries are contained in F. S. Regs., Part II. and the Staff Manual respectively. Title Pages will be prepared in manuscript.

Place	Date	Hour	Summary of Events and Information	Remarks and references to Appendices
OTTAWA	April 1917. 29		Interior economy and refitting under Coy. arrangements.	
	30		Platoon training and tactical exercise.	
	31st May 1917.			

H.V.Kemsle
Lieut. Colonel
Cmdg 1/23rd Bn. The London Regt.

Army Form C. 2118.

WAR DIARY
INTELLIGENCE SUMMARY.
(Erase heading not required.)

Place	Date	Hour	Summary of Events and Information	Remarks and references to Appendices
OTTAWA	May 1917			
	1	6.15 am	Roll Call. 8.30 - 12.30 - Coy Specialist Training.	
		11.30 - 2.30 pm	D & C Coy went up with details to bethe at MOROUTRE.	
	2	6.15	Roll Call. 9 - 12.30 Coy Specialist Training	
		3.30 PM	Platoon Commanders under Capt R.H. TOLERTON, carried out Tactical Exercise	
		2-4.30	Bathing at MOROUTRE	
	3	6.30	Battn. Roll Call.	
		8.30 - 12.30	Coy Specialist Training. Bombers on Bn Bomb Course. Lewis Gunners on L.G. range	
	4	6.15	Battn. Roll Call. 8.45 - 12.30 Bn Training	
		1.30	Platoon Commanders carried out Tactical Exercise under Capt TOLERTON	
	5	6.30	Battn. Roll Call. 8.30 - 12.30 Coy Specialist Training.	
			Rifle Range at disposal of Bn. 9 AM - 1 PM - used for L.G. practice.	
	6	10 AM	Parade Service.	
		11	Inspection of Camp by Commanding Officer.	
			Bn relieved 24th Bn Ln Regt in Right Sector, CANAL Sub Sector, YPRES. A Coy Left, C Coy Right, supporting line, B Coy support, D Coy Reserve. HQ in BLUFF TUNNELS.	
			Night firing carried out.	
			5 O.R. wounded during relief.	

Army Form C. 2118.

123rd BATTN.
THE LOGON
REGIMENT.

WAR DIARY
or
INTELLIGENCE SUMMARY.
(Erase heading not required.)

Instructions regarding War Diaries and Intelligence
Summaries are contained in F. S. Regs., Part II.
and the Staff Manual respectively. Title pages
will be prepared in manuscript.

Place	Date	Hour	Summary of Events and Information	Remarks and references to Appendices
CANAL Left Sector	7		1 OR Wounded	
	8	6.15	—	
	10th		3.15 P.M. & 11. S.O.S. sent up by 19th Devon (on right) as enemy were putting up heavy barrage. Our artillery opened fire and enemy fire slackened down 4.30 P.M. Our casualties 5 O.R. "D" relieved A and B relieved "C" Coy.	
	12		1 OR Killed	
	14		Bn. relieved by 24th Bn. Londons and marched to OTTAWA Camp	
OTTAWA	15		Interior Economy etc	
	16		Bn. bathed at HONDUTRE. 9.30 A.M. 1 Officer + 1 N.C.O. per Coy under Major HARGREAVES. D.S.O. [Tactical training]	
	17	6.30	Bn. Roll Call Parade	
		9 A.M.	Batt. Drill — Training until 12.30 P.M.	
		2.15 P.M.	Lecture by Commanding Officer to all Officers & N.C.Os	
	18		Parades as for 17th	
	19	8.45 A.M.	Bn. paraded and marched to STEENVOORDE Training Area	
	20	10 A.M.	Attack practice	
	21	"	"	

WAR DIARY
or
INTELLIGENCE SUMMARY.
(Erase heading not required.)

Army Form C. 2118.

Instructions regarding War Diaries and Intelligence Summaries are contained in F.S. Regs., Part II. and the Staff Manual respectively. Title pages will be prepared in manuscript.

Place	Date	Hour	Summary of Events and Information	Remarks and references to Appendices
STEENVOORDE	22	6.10	Roll Call parade	
		9.30	Attack practice	
	23	6.10	Roll Call	
		9.30	Attack Practice. Divine fighting Order. Toe lines paraded with Bn.	
	24	9.30	" "	
		11.15pm	Bn. marched to GODEWAERSVELDE, entrained & over POPERINGHE, marched to OTTAWA	
	25		Transport marched by road.	
	26		Bn. relieved 19th Bn Lon Regt in Right Section Canal Bk Sector. Draft C joined Ransfort, Reserve	
	28		1 OR wounded	
	29		3 " "	
	30		A relieved B, B relieved "C" Cy	
	31		1 OR killed, 5 OR wounded	
			5 " wounded. Bn relieved by 20th Bn London Regt and marched to CANAL RESERVE CAMP	

1/23RD BATTN.
THE LONDON
REGIMENT.

No.
Date 6-6-17

H H Kemble Lieut Colonel
Cmdg 1/23rd Bn The London Regiment

WAR DIARY or INTELLIGENCE SUMMARY

Army Form C. 2118.

THE LONDON REGIMENT.

1/23

Place	Date	Hour	Summary of Events and Information	Remarks and references to Appendices
	June 1917			
CANAL RESERVE CAMP	1		Bn marched to DEVONSHIRE Camp and slept in bivouac.	
DEVONSHIRE	2		Interior economy & refitting.	
	3	7am–8.30pm	B & D Coys MOD bathed at HALIFAX.	
		10 PM	Church Parade in Canteen.	
	4	10 AM	Lecture by C.O. to A & B; 11 PM to C & D Coys.	
	5	3.30 PM	Bn paraded and marched to CANAL RESERVE Camp; thence at 10 PM to BLUFF TUNNELS.	APPENDIX I
Right Section CANAL SubSector YPRES	7		Bn. in attack on YPRES - COMINES Canal. Lt. Col. H.A. KEMBLE, D.S.O., M.C., Died of wounds. 1/Lts L.P CLIFFORD, H. STONE and G.W FRANKLYN killed in action. Major T.C. HARGREAVES, D.S.O. assumed command of Bn.	
	9/10		Bn HQ moved back to BLUFF TUNNELS. Total Casualties (O.R.) 33 Killed 159 Wounded 2 missing.	
	12	10 PM	Bn marched to KEMPTON PARK, WESTOUTRE.	
KEMPTON PARK	13		Resting.	
	14	10 PM	Battn addressed by B.G.C. 142nd Infantry Brigade.	
	15	4.30 PM	Bn marched to CAESTRE and billeted in camp.	
CAESTRE		7.30 AM	" " " to RACQUINGHEM, arriving at 3 pm and billeted.	
RACQUINGHEM	17	10 AM	Church Parade.	

1/23RD BATTN.,
THE LONDON
REGIMENT.

Army Form C. 2118.

WAR DIARY
or
INTELLIGENCE SUMMARY.
(Erase heading not required.)

Instructions regarding War Diaries and Intelligence Summaries are contained in F.S. Regs., Part II. and the Staff Manual respectively. Title pages will be prepared in manuscript.

Place	Date	Hour	Summary of Events and Information	Remarks and references to Appendices
	June 1917			
RACQUINGHEM	17	6.30 PM	Bn. paraded & marched to ST MARTIN-AU-LAERT, via ST OMER, arriving 9.15 PM	
ST MARTIN	18	11-12	Section Platoon drill. Musketry programme postponed on account of bad weather	
	19	9 AM - 12 noon	Coys. on "D" Range at CORMETTE, B, C, D, A - 45 minutes per Coy	
	20	9 AM - 10.30	Musketry instruction. L.G. instruction for untrained men.	
		12 noon - 3 p.m.	Coys. on Range at CORMETTE, D, C, B - A on duty on Range	
	21	9 AM	A, C, D - B " "	
		12 noon		
		2.30 - 4 p.m.	Musketry Instruction under Coy. arrangements.	
	22	9.30 AM	Battalion Parade.	
		12 noon	Companies on Range - C Coy. on duty.	
		2-3 p.m.	Lewis guns on miniature range	
	23	9 AM	Battalion Parade.	
		9.20 - 10.45	Musketry Instruction by Coys. 2-5 p.m. Companies on Range - D on duty	
		7 p.m.	Battn. paraded and marched to RACQUINGHEM, arriving about 9.45 p.m.	
RACQUINGHEM	24	10.35 PM	Parade Service. Medal ribbons presented by G.O.C. 47th (London) Division, up to date awarded	
			Awards for the action on June 9th & 9th :- 3 Military Cross, 6 ; D.C.M., 3 Military	
			Medal, 19 (including men attached to M.G. Coy and T.M.B.)	

Army Form C. 2118.

1/23RD BATTN.,
THE LONDON REGIMENT.

No.............
Date...........

WAR DIARY
or
INTELLIGENCE SUMMARY.
(Erase heading not required.)

Instructions regarding War Diaries and Intelligence Summaries are contained in F. S. Regs., Part II. and the Staff Manual respectively. Title pages will be prepared in manuscript.

Place	Date	Hour	Summary of Events and Information	Remarks and references to Appendices
	June 1917			
RACQUINGHEM	25	9.15 A AM-PM	Bn parade. 10-12.30 Peloton drill, platoon in attack, & musketry instruction. 2.15-3.15 Coy lectures	
	26	9 AM	" " 10-12. Close order " " "	
			Divisional Sports at BLARINGHEM.	
	27	6.15 AM	A, D and C & S Coys left in motor lorries for SERCUS; thence by march route to METEREN.	
		7.30	A & B Coys left in motor lorries for HAZEBROUCK " " "	
METEREN	28	5.30 AM	Bn paraded and marched to RIDGE WOOD. Lt Col A. MAXWELL, D.S.O, 1/6th Bn London Regt joined and resumed command of Bn. Battn in bivouacs & dugouts.	
RIDGE WOOD	29	2.30-4.30 PM	Commanding Officer inspects Camp & H.Q. details (each separately) in F.M.O.	
		7.45 PM	Bn moved to DAMMSTRASSE area.	
DAMMSTRASSE	30	9 PM	Bn moved into Bde Support, relieving 20th D.L.I. Disposition:- H right Coy: B A. Left Coy B. Support Coy C. Reserve Co D. 22nd Bn on right of Bn. 72nd Bde across canal on left of Bn.	Personnel etc.

T2134. Wt. W708-776. 500/000. 4/15. Sir J. C. & S.

NARRATIVE

of 2nd Army Offensive Operations
of June 7th – 9th 1917
as far as they concerned the
1/23 Bn The London Regt.

Refce
47th Dist. map.
3a.

APPENDIX
to WAR DIARY
for June 1917.

June 7th — At 3.9 a.m. the Hill 60 mines were sprung and at 3.10 a.m. those under ST ELOI. Our guns opened instantly and heavily. It was noticeable that though the German guns did not fire for some time, the machine gun at O.5.a.50.05 opened fire immediately. There appeared to be little retaliation from the enemy guns, and the Battalion was enabled to assemble in front of RENNIE ST in snake formation, by half platoons, without molestation. The right flank consisted of 'A' Coy followed by 'D' Company, and the left flank by 'B' Coy followed by 'C' Coy. A Vickers gun went with each of the rear company commanders.

The Commanding Officer [Lt. Col. H. H. Kemble D.S.O., M.C.] insisted on accompanying the Battalion as far as O.B.1. where the four waves were formed. On returning after seeing them leave O.B.1. he was mortally wounded by a shrapnel bullet in the chest, in HEDGE ROW.

Bn. Hdqrs were shared with the 1/24th Bn, and between 4.0 a.m. and 5.0 a.m. Lt. Col. Milner interviewed several prisoners there. From these valuable information was received regarding the enemy's dispositions and intentions – namely the light holding of the front trench with reserve companies one kilometre back, and the absence of booby traps.

At 4.35 a.m. the battalion crossed no mans land in waves and by 6.0 a.m. search in the meanwhile having proved fruitless, the Colonel's absence was reported. It was learned shortly afterwards that he had been wounded, and Major. T.C. Hargreaves D.S.O. assumed command. The signal officer [Lieut W. Lewis] had been detached for duty for several hours in connexion with Added Bde Report Centre, and it was about 6.0 a.m. that a report was received by wire that he had got into the German trenches before the assaulting waves of another Battalion and taken officers and men prisoners.

The Battalion reached the Blue Line with but few casualties, and again reorganised here.

From this point the assaults on the four objectives were carried out exactly according to operation orders, our artillery fire being so accurate that the battalion was able to advance less that 50 yards behind the barrage. The only deviation from the schedule was that 'A' company crossed the CANAL a little too far to the right, losing touch with 'B' company for a short period.

At 8.5 am a message was received that this side of the SPOIL BANK [in O.5.a] was in our hands; and between 8.0 am and 9 am about 50 prisoners came down from this vicinity.
When information was received that the crossing of the canal had been effected, permission was asked of Bde. to move Bn HQrs forward. This was granted and at 9.15 am Bn HQrs moved forward, halting in O.G.2. Here a good dugout was discovered at I.34.d.20.10 and here a Bn Hdqrs was organised, runners, telephones etc being sent out to reconnoitre the proposed Hdqrs at O.4.6.7.5.
When that was reported to be non-existent Bn. H.Q. was definitely established at I.34.d.20.10. and a report rendered to that effect to Brigade at 10.45 am by which hour communication by wire was established both with the BLUFF and SPOIL BANK. By 11.0 am touch by wire and runner was established with O.C./101st Bn. on the left flank, who was held up and who asked for assistance.
At 11.40 am the ration Officer 2/Lt. A.W. Durrant arrived from the Brown Hdqrs with messages from OC. B'day timed 8.0 am. and announcing the capture of prisoners, 2 minenwerfer with ammunition and a machine gun with much ammunition which had straightway been turned on the enemy. Meanwhile C & D companies had crossed the canal. The crossing was carried out in file with little difficulty and few casualties. By 9.0 am these companies were established in OPAL RESERVE, and the work of consolidation had begun. 'D' Coy was in touch with the 76th Bn on the right, but the entire left flank consisting of 'C' Company and 'B' Coy - [who were realising the situation were forming a defensive flank of posts on the E slope of SPOIL BANK] - was exposed. O.C. C company dug a trench with the 101st Bn; but, failing to do this, protected his flank with 2 Lewis Guns and the Vickers gun which had come up with him & which was subsequently put out of action.
During the advance there was little hand to hand fighting. The enemy surrendered freely wherever encountered, and apart from desultory shelling the only hindrance was from snipers whose efforts were partially neutralised by those of the snipers attached to our own companies.
From noon onwards the enemy shelled more heavily but no immediate counter attack was attempted. The time for the SECOND ZERO was received soon after 1. p.m. The companies were warned, and O.C. 'D' Coy sent out a N.C.O. to reconnoitre the hedge in front of OPTIC TRENCH. He got within 10 yards of the hedge and found that underneath it was an occupied dugout [from which a machine gun later opened fire]. There appeared to be little wire in front of OPTIC TRENCH.
At 5.45 pm the Intelligence Officer was sent round to companies to warn them to expect a counter attack during the night.

At 5.30 pm a wire was received from Bde to the effect that the Germans had been "seen, by aeroplanes, in force at 4.0 pm near KORTEWILDE, and moving in our direction.

The attack of the /20th Bn on the LONG SPOIL BANK was timed for 7.0 pm. The barrage for this appeared to coincide with the German barrage for their attempted counter attack, and the gun fire was very heavy. Before 8.0 pm the attack of the /20th Bn had failed, and before 8.30 pm the enemy were again in occupation of the LONG SPOIL BANK. The enemy were now observed trying to move from OBLIQUE ROW and OBLIQUE TRENCH, and their barrage being heavy the S.O.S. signal was fired and our guns prevented them leaving their trenches. It was some hours before the gun fire died down, and the rest of the night was quiet.

During
JUNE 8th Consolidation was carried on. Supplies were carried up and dumps formed, men were reorganised, and burial and stretcher bearer parties cleared the Area, both N. & S. of the canal, of dead and wounded.

For some hours we had the assistance of 2 officers and several men of the /20th Bn. who found themselves in the area of our left front line company. During the day the enemy began to establish himself in the trenches opposite our own, and movement across the canal and over the open to OPAL RESERVE became increasingly difficult by reason of the fire of snipers and machine guns.

About 7.30 pm the enemy put up an intense barrage on this trench and on the SPOIL BANK. Casualties were caused, the trench damaged and the remaining Vickers gun put out of action. The S.O.S. signal was sent up on both flanks & repeated by us. There was an intense reciprocal barrage during which no. 6 platoon under Sgt Worsfold made a gallant effort to reinforce OPAL RESERVE across the canal but was unable to do so, Sgt Worsfold himself being severely wounded.

No enemy were observed to leave their trenches, but it was not until 11 pm that the barrage died down.

During all this time telephone communication was only once interrupted and then only for a few minutes when lamp signalling proved an efficient substitute. In the evening the 1st 7th Bn relieved the bays S. of the Canal, relief being complete at 3.20 am.

On the morning of
JUNE 9th OC "B" Coy sent out an N.C.O. and 2 men to patrol the LONG SPOIL BANK on the Canal side. 150ᵈˢ was patrolled dugouts and tunnels entered and a telephone disconnected

without any opposition being encountered.

At 7.0 p.m. the same evening C.S.M. Dachter of "B" Coy repeated the enterprise, again meeting no opposition.

Except for desultory bombardments the day passed quietly, and early next morning Bn. H.Q. and the SPOIL BANK were taken over by the 18th Bn, relief being completed at 1.30. a.m.

The Stokes Mortars were unable to take a very active part in the operations.

During the whole operation, the front line and supporting troops were continually supplied with S.A.A., Bombs, Water, Rations and Hot Tea. In all 2320 pints of hot tea were issued and 176 2gallon tins of water were sent up.

Reports from Signal Officer and Intelligence Officer are appended.

(Sd) J. C. Hargreaves. Major
Comdg. 23 Bn The London Regt.

Countersigned
Armawell
Lt Col.

Army Form C. 2118.

WAR DIARY
~~INTELLIGENCE SUMMARY~~

Instructions regarding War Diaries and Intelligence Summaries are contained in F.S. Regs., Part II. and the Staff Manual respectively. Title pages will be prepared in manuscript.

(Erase heading not required.)

1/23 London
1 5 29

Place	Date	Hour	Summary of Events and Information	Remarks and references to Appendices
Trenches immediately S. of YPRES. CANAL.	JULY 1917. 1		2/Lt C.I. Mansel-Howe Wounded. 1 O.R. Killed (S.I.W.) and 3 O.R. wounded.	
	2	2 AM	2 prisoners 12th Co. 8th Bav. R.I.R. brought in. 3 O.R. killed, 11 wounded	
	3		D relieved A, C relieved B Coys. 2 O.R. wounded.	
	4		1 O.R. killed; 2/Lt K.I. NEWELL and 20 O.R. wounded.	
	5		2/Lt A.M. Mitchell MC Killed; 2 O.R. killed and 4 O.R. wounded.	
	6 7		3 O.R. wounded and 1 Missing (700515 Cpl C.G. Guille)	
	8		Bn relieved by 8th Bn Lon Regt. and marched to Camp at M,6.d.5.8. (28 S.W.5A 1/20,000)	
M,6.d.5.8.	9		Interior economy. Major T.C. Hargreaves DSO to Hospital (sick).	
	10	AM	" " 2.30 P.M. G.O. inspected Camp.	
	11	8.30	Physical and close order drill. 10 AM. Musketry & Bayonet Fighting. Specialists under Specialist Officers. 2/Lts F.B. ALLEN and C.M. WHEELER joined from Base.	
	12		4 Officers 200 O.R. working party at Brigade School enlarging rifle range. 2/Lt J.S. MOLLER sick to Hospital.	
	13	AM 8.30	Physical & close order drill. 10 AM Musketry & Bayonet fighting.	
	14		Bn inspected by Divl. Commander.	
	15		Church Parade. Bn moved into Support in Left Section, CANAL Sub-Sector, relieving 1/17th	

Army Form C. 2118.

WAR DIARY
or
INTELLIGENCE SUMMARY.
(Erase heading not required.)

Instructions regarding War Diaries and Intelligence Summaries are contained in F. S. Regs., Part II. and the Staff Manual respectively. Title pages will be prepared in manuscript.

Place	Date	Hour	Summary of Events and Information	Remarks and references to Appendices
SUPPORT	15		Bn The London Regt. H.Q. and C Coy in BLUFF TUNNELS, A B & D in RAVINE. 3 O.R. Wounded.	
	18		1 O.R. Killed.	
	19		" Wounded, 8 O.R. wounded at duty, all caused by a new "mustard-oil" German gas shell.	
	20		2 " 2/Lt. A.G. BROWN joined from Base.	
	21		Relieved 1/24th Bn London Regt. in front line, Right section, BATTLE WOOD Sub-Sector. A & B front line, D support in RAT ALLEY, C- Reserve in BLUFF TUNNELS. H.Q. in IMPERIAL SUPPORT trench. 1 O.R. wounded.	
	22		6 O.R. wounded, 1 O.R. wounded at duty.	
	23		1 O.R. Killed.	
	24		4 " wounded, 2 O.R. wounded at duty.	
	25		2 " " Bn. relieved by 11th Bn Queen's R.W.S. and marched to KEMPTON CAMP, WESTOUTRE. 1 " Missing (702796 Pte F.C. Littlewood).	
	26		Refitting.	
	27	AM 10	Div. Commander inspected Camp. Bn bathed at WESTOUTRE.	
	28	8.30	Training under Coy. arrangements. 2/Lts C.R.ALDRICH and A.P.CHURCH joined from Base. 6 Officers proceeded on leave to U.K.	

Army Form C. 2118.

WAR DIARY
or
INTELLIGENCE SUMMARY.
(Erase heading not required.)

Instructions regarding War Diaries and Intelligence Summaries are contained in F.S. Regs., Part II. and the Staff Manual respectively. Title pages will be prepared in manuscript.

Place	Date	Hour	Summary of Events and Information	Remarks and references to Appendices
KEMPTON CAMP.	29	9.30	Combined Church Parade with 24th Bn Lon. Regt. Lt. Col. A. MAXWELL DSO proceeded on leave to U.K. Capt. R.H. TOLERTON MC assumed command of Battalion.	
	30	11.30	Training under Coy. arrangements (delayed on account of rain).	
	31	11	Bn inspected by Brigadier, 142 Inf Bde., who presented Bars to M.M., and afterwards inspected Transport. Specialist Training under Specialist Officers.	

1.8.17.

[signature] Captain,

Commanding, 1/23rd Battalion The London Regiment, T.F.

Army Form C. 2118.

WAR DIARY
of
INTELLIGENCE SUMMARY.
(Erase heading not required.)

1/23rd Bn The London Regt. T.F.

Instructions regarding War Diaries and Intelligence Summaries are contained in F. S. Regs., Part II. and the Staff Manual respectively. Title pages will be prepared in manuscript.

Place	Date	Hour	Summary of Events and Information	Remarks and references to Appendices
August, 1917.				
KEMPTON PARK	1	8.30 a.m.	Close order & physical drill. Specialists under Specialist Officers.	
"		2.30 p.m.	Coy. classes in map reading, message writing, etc.	
"	2	8.30 a.m.	Training as above.	
"	3	8.30	Training as above. Route marches by Companies.	
"	4	8.30 a.m.	Coy. and Specialist training. 11.30 AM to 4.30 PM, Bn bathed at WESTOUTRE baths.	
"	5	9.50 a.m.	Church parade. Lt D.J. WARDLEY, MC, appt'd Adjutant as from 7/2/17. 2/Lt G.K.G. BETTANY appt'd Transport Officer.	
"	6	8.30	Coy and Specialist Training till 12 noon.	
"	7	8.30 "	" " AM	
"	8	8.30 - 10.30.	" " PM Coy training. 10.15 - 3.15 Companies on range at M.4.c.4.0.	
"	9		Bn entrained at POPERINGHE for ST OMER; marched to ZUDAUSQUES and billeted.	
ZUDAUSQUES	10		Interior economy.	
"	11	7.45	Bn paraded and marched to Range. D Coy on duty in Butts. Firing 9 a.m. to 1.45 p.m.	
"	12		Church parade. Inspection of billets by Commanding Officer.	
"	13	8.15	Batt'n. parade and training.	
"	14	"	Battalion drill, Coy. drill and Specialist training.	
"		2 pm	Battalion inspected by Gen. Sir H. PLUMER, Comdg. Second Army.	

Army Form C. 2118.

WAR DIARY
or
INTELLIGENCE SUMMARY.
(Erase heading not required.)

1/23rd Bn The London Regt. T.F.

Instructions regarding War Diaries and Intelligence Summaries are contained in F. S. Regs., Part II. and the Staff Manual respectively. Title pages will be prepared in manuscript.

Place	Date	Hour	Summary of Events and Information	Remarks and references to Appendices
AUGUST, 1917.				
ZUDAUSQUES	15	8.15	Battn. Parade. Extended order drill, musketry, judging distances, etc.	
"	16	9 pm	Night scheme by Platoon Commanders.	
"	17	9.15	P.T. and B.F. 10.15. Practise attack. P.m. 2.30 Specialist training.	
"			Bn. marched to WIZERNES and entrained for OUDERDOM, thence to DOMINION CAMP. Transport marched independently.	
DOMINION.	19	9 am	Training under Coy. arrangements until 10.30. Voluntary service at 9.30	
"	20		Bn marched to SWAN CHATEAU (in reserve) relieving 2nd Devons and 2nd W. Yorks.	
SWAN CHATEAU	21		Training under Coy. arrangements in Lewis Gun, bombing, musketry, etc.	
"	24		Bn moved up to front line on WESTHOEK ridge, relieving 9th Bn K.R.R.C. C Coy left, A right, firing line, B Coy support, D Coy reserve (in HOOGE). Casualties: 4 O.R. wounded.	
WESTHOEK	25		Shell entered and exploded inside Headquarters Dugout, killing 2 O.R. and wounding 6 O.R. Other casualties, 4 O.R. wounded.	
"	26		Bn. relieved by 8th Bn London Regt. and withdrew to reserve in RAILWAY WOOD tunnels.	
"	27		Casualties: 6 O.R. wounded.	
"	28		Bn moved up to WESTHOEK RIDGE, relieving 24th Bn London Regt., in centre of Divisional front. B Coy left, D Coy right, firing line. A & C in close support. Bn H.Q. on RIDGE. Casualties, 5 O.R. wounded.	

Army Form C. 2118.

WAR DIARY
or
INTELLIGENCE SUMMARY.
(Erase heading not required.)

1/23rd Bn. The London Regt. T.F.

Place	Date	Hour	Summary of Events and Information	Remarks and references to Appendices
AUGUST, 1917.				
	29		2 German prisoners brought in by "D" Company. Casualties, 3 O.R. wounded.	
	30		Casualties, 4 O.R. wounded.	
	31		" 4 O.R. "	
2/9/17.				

[signature] Lieut. Colonel,
Commanding, 1/23rd Battn. The London Regiment.

Army Form C. 2118.

WAR DIARY
of
INTELLIGENCE SUMMARY
(Erase heading not required.)

1/23rd Battn The London Regt. T.F.

Instructions regarding War Diaries and Intelligence Summaries are contained in F.S. Regs., Part II. and the Staff Manual respectively. Title pages will be prepared in manuscript.

Vol 31

145/47

Place	Date	Hour	Summary of Events and Information	Remarks and references to Appendices
	SEPTEMBER, 1917.			
	1		Battalion in line.	
	2		Battn. relieved by 2nd Bn Royal Irish Rifles and marched to DOMINION CAMP. 2/Lt A.P.CHURCH Wd.	
DOMINION	4	a.m.	" bathed at HALIFAX Baths.	
	5	9.25	" marched to STEENVOORDE. Bt. A.C.P.R. WEST joined from Base, with 18 O.R.	
STEENVOORDE	6		Refitting and Reorganisation.	
	7	9	Physical training, Musketry, close order drill. Capt. H.B.N. NIXON from Hospital.	
	8	9 - 11.30	Training as for 7th inst. 2/Lt J.M. HUMPHRIES joined from Base.	
	9		Battalion Sports Day. 7 O.R. from Base.	
	9	11	Parade Service.	
	10	7	Battn. paraded and proceeded by motor buses to HALIFAX Camp, thence to DICKEBUSH HUTS by march route. Transport marched independently, leaving at 8.15 a.m.	
DICKEBUSH	11	a.m	Close order drill, physical training, musketry and gas drill.	
	12	a.m.	Training as 11th inst. Training of Reserve S.B., Bombers, etc. 200 O.R. carrying Gas Cylinders to WESTHOEK RIDGE.	
	13	a.m.	" 12th " 11 O.R. from Base. Party of 100 O.R. burying cable.	
	14	9 "	Close order drill, P.T. & B.F., musketry and passing of messages.	
	15	9 "	Training as for 14th inst. Bathing at HALIFAX Baths.	

Army Form C. 2118.

WAR DIARY
or
INTELLIGENCE SUMMARY.

(Erase heading not required.)

1/23rd Battn. The London Regt.

Instructions regarding War Diaries and Intelligence Summaries are contained in F. S. Regs., Part II. and the Staff Manual respectively. Title pages will be prepared in manuscript.

Place	Date	Hour	Summary of Events and Information	Remarks and references to Appendices
	SEPTEMBER, 1917.			
DICKEBUSCH	16	a.m. 7.50	Battn. marched to VANOOST CAMP, WIPPENHOEK.	
VANOOST	17		Training under Coy. arrangements. Capt. F. ENTWISLE, M.C., to Hospital.	
	18	a.m. 10.45	Battn. marched to STEENVOORDE area and billeted.	
STEENVOORDE	19		Training under Coy. arrangements.	
	20		Commanding Officer inspected Companies and Details. Training as 19th inst. 51 O.R. from Base.	
	21		One hour's training.	
	22	a.m. 1.15	Bn. marched to BAVINCHOVE Stn. and entrained.	
	23	p.m. 12.45	Bn. detrained at MAROEUIL, near ARRAS, entrained on Light Railway and detrained at WAKEFIELD CAMP.	
WAKEFIELD CAMP	23		Training under Coy. arrangements.	
	24	8.15	Bn. paraded and marched to Railway Cutting (H.Q. B.21.c.6.2 - Sheet 51 b 1/20,000) relieving ANSON Battn. 63rd (Naval) Division in reserve to Left Section, OPPY Front sector.	
OPPY front.	25 – 30th.		Battn. found working parties day and night (in all, 200 O.R.) on pipe line, building Strong Posts, etc. 2/Lt. J.H. HORNBY joined from Base 20 29/9/17.	

1.10.1917.

[signature] Lieut. Colonel,

Commanding, 1/23rd Battalion The London Regiment, T.F.

Army Form C. 2118.

WAR DIARY
or
INTELLIGENCE SUMMARY
(Erase heading not required.) 1/23rd Battn. The London Regt.

Wd 32

Place	Date	Hour	Summary of Events and Information	Remarks and references to Appendices
RAILWAY CUTTING.	OCTOBER 1917		2/Lt K.N. HONEYMAN joined from Base.	
	2		Bn relieved 1/24th Bn London Regt. in right (R.3) section of Brigade front. A, C, D Front line, B Coy insupport.	
	5		2/Lt E.J. HOLTHAM wounded.	
	9		2 O.R. Killed, 3 O.R. wounded by "pineapple" bomb.	
	10		Bn. relieved by 7th Bn London Regt. and proceeded by Light Railway to ST AUBIN.	
ST AUBIN	11		Interior economy. 701788 Pte C. FRANKLIN Accidentally killed.	
	12	9 AM	Close order drill, physical training, musketry. Each Coy. on Assault course for 45 minutes.	
	13	9 AM	P.T. and B.F. Route marches by Companies.	
	14	9.15 A.M.	Parade Service. 2 Officers & 100 O.R. burying cable.	
	15	8.30 A.M.	A & C carried out special training. B & D Coys. on Range.	
	16	8.30 A.M.	D, B and H.Q. Details bathed at ANZIN. 2/Lt. C.W. WALKER from Base.	
	16	8.30 A.M.	A, B & C Coys. carried out attack practice. D Coy trained under Coy. arrangements.	
	17	8.45	" Training as for yesterday.	
	18		Bn relieved 19th Bn London Regt in support in GAVRELLE sector. A & B in NAVAL TRENCH, C & D in RED LINE.	
GAVRELLE	21		Lieut. A.J. HARMAN FROM Base. Major T.C. HARGREAVES, DSO, assumed Command of Bn.	
	26		Bn relieved 24th Battn. London Regt! in front line: D and C front line, B Coy Support, A Coy. reserve.	

2449 Wt. W14957/M90 750,000 1/16 J.B.C. & A. Forms/C.2118/12.

Army Form C. 2118.

WAR DIARY
INTELLIGENCE SUMMARY
(Erase heading not required.)

Instructions regarding War Diaries and Intelligence Summaries are contained in F. S. Regs., Part II. and the Staff Manual respectively. Title Pages will be prepared in manuscript.

Place	Date	Hour	Summary of Events and Information	Remarks and references to Appendices
	OCTOBER 1917.			
	30		B relieved C Coy. in front line. A and C Coys, with half of Hqrs., relieved by 2 Companies and half Hqrs 1/24th Bn. London Regt. for purpose of practising raid. Bn billeted in ANZIN.	
	31	5 p.m	A & C Coys and Hqrs. moved to ST AUBIN and billeted.	
	2/11/17.			

Shakespeare, Major,

Commanding, 1/23rd Battn. The London Regiment.

Army Form C. 2118.

WAR DIARY
or
INTELLIGENCE SUMMARY

(Erase heading not required.)

1/23rd Bn. The London Regt. T.F.

Instructions regarding War Diaries and Intelligence Summaries are contained in F.S. Regs., Part II. and the Staff Manual respectively. Title Pages will be prepared in manuscript.

Place	Date November 1917	Hour	Summary of Events and Information	Remarks and references to Appendices
ST. AUBIN	1	8 AM	A.v.C. Bn. practised Raid on prepared course. Lt. J.G. GARTHWAITE joined from Base.	
	2	9.30 "	" "	
	3	8.30 am	Bn. paraded and proceeded by Light Railway to GAVRELLE SECTOR.	
GAVRELLE	4	4.30 pm	A & C Companies raided German trenches (in conjunction with 1/24 Bn. Lon Regt.). Casualties :- 2/Lt. A.W. TUGWELL wounded, 2 O.R. killed and 19 O.R. wounded.	Report attached
	5	11 AM	Bn. relieved and marched to AUBREY Camp.	
AUBREY	6	P.M. 2.45	Bn. inspected by Army Commander. Bathed at ROCLINCOURT.	
	7	AM. PM. 8.30 - 11.15	Bn. on Range.	
	8	AM 9.30	Route marches by Companies in fighting order.	
	9	am 8.30 - 1 pm.	Bn. on Range at MAROEUIL. Companies on Butt duty when not firing.	
	10	am 8.30	Rifles inspected by Armr. Sergt. Route marches by Companies.	
	11	am 10.30	Parade Service. Interior Economy.	
	12	—	Training under Coy. arrangements; Bombing, L.G., and Physical exercises	

Army Form C. 2118.

WAR DIARY
or
INTELLIGENCE SUMMARY

(Erase heading not required.) 1/23rd Bn. The London Regt. T.F.

Place	Date	Hour	Summary of Events and Information	Remarks and references to Appendices
	November 1917			
AUBREY	13	11.45 am	Bn. paraded and marched to R.2 Sub-Sector, OPPY, relieving 8th Bn. Lon. Regt. A Coy Right, B Coy Left, front line; C Coy Support; D Coy Reserve.	
	18		Draft of 28 O.Rs from Base.	
	19	9.30 am	Bn. relieved by 11th Bn. E. Yorks Regt. (21st Division) and marched to AUBREY Camp.	
AUBREY	20	12.50 pm	Bn. bathed at St CATHERINES. Bn. refitted.	
	21	9.30 am	Awards of 6 M.Ms and 1 bar to M.M. in connection with raid on 11th inst. announced.	
		8.25 am	Bn. paraded and marched to LE PENDU Camp, near MONT ST ÉLOY. 8 O.Rs from Base.	
LE PENDU	22	9.15 am	" " BIRNEVILLE.	
BIRNEVILLE	23		Bn. rested and cleaned up. Awards of 3 M.C.s (Capt. G.A. BRETT, Capt. G.E. PALMER, & Lt. W.E. PHILLIPS) 2 D.C.Ms and 2 M.M.s, in connection with raid on 11th inst. announced.	
	24	7.30 am	Bn. paraded and marched to GOMIECOURT, & billeted under canvas. The weather was very rough and the wind high; many tents were blown down.	
GOMIECOURT	25	1.15 pm	Bn. paraded and marched to Nissen hut camp at BARASTRE, via BAPAUME.	
BARASTRE	26		Interior economy. Major W.H. MURPHY, 1/8th Bn. The London Regt., assumed command of Bn. vice Major F.C. Hargreaves, D.S.O.	

Army Form C. 2118.

WAR DIARY
or
INTELLIGENCE SUMMARY

(Erase heading not required.)

Instructions regarding War Diaries and Intelligence Summaries are contained in F. S. Regs., Part II. and the Staff Manual respectively. Title Pages will be prepared in manuscript.

Place	Date	Hour	Summary of Events and Information	Remarks and references to Appendices
	November 1917			
BAPAUME	27	1 pm	Bn. marched to camp near BEAUMETZ-Les-CAMBRAI and billetted in tents.	
BEAUMETZ	29		Bn. moved to HINDENBURG support to K.10.d.	
	29		Bn. moved to HINDENBURG LINE in K.9.	
Fontaine Res.	30		Heavy enemy attack between MOEUVRES and FONTAINE. Bn. standing by ready to reinforce. Bn. much reinforced defensive position in K.8.d. and K.9.a. moved to K.10 between K 28.C and K.3.6. and to 10 pm had relieved 13 K.R.R.C. in front line between K.22.c. 9.6. 15 and K.27. to 5.4. (at 11.30 pm orders were received that Bn. was being relieved immediately by 1st K.R.R.C. Relief completed by 4 am Dec 1st)	

Casly 23rd B. The ?
[illegible signature]

Report on Raid
carried out by 1/23rd Bn. The London Regt.
in conjunction with 1/24th Bn. The London Regt.,
in the GAVRELLE sub-sector at 4.30 p.m. 4th Nov. 1917.
-o-o-o-o-o-o-o-o-o-o-

A. NARRATIVE.

The Raiding Companies were assembled in the British Front Line by 4.10 p.m. and a rum issue was then made. Each section was definitely allotted to one of the 11 gaps which had been previously cut, by the garrison, in our wire, and opposite to which small boards numbered G.0 to G.11 had been fixed in the parados and steps made up the parapet. There was no difficulty in getting out of our front line and forming up into waves outside our wire.

At ZERO minus 30 seconds several field guns and one or two machine guns opened fire on the left of the first objective; and at 4.30 p.m. sharp all the other artillery, machine guns, etc., opened up. The barrage throughout was perfect except for a shortness of about 40 yards on the left; but this was not dangerous for the line was always clearly defined.

The assault proceeded according to plan. The enemy machine gun in GAVRELLE TRENCH, just North of CARP, opened fire while the Raiders were crossing No Man's Land but the shooting was wild and caused no casualties. This gun soon ceased fire, being caught in our barrage, and was afterwards captured. A second machine gun fired from GAVRELLE SUPPORT on the second wave between GAVRELLE TRENCH and CRAP, but the fire was erratic and high and caused practically no casualties.

There was some opposition in both objectives but many of the enemy left their trenches and ran back. In the first line a party at the head of CARP showed fight; the second wave, however, drove them down CARP and eventually killed them with bombs. An enemy machine gun was also taken here and the crew killed with bombs.

In the second line the only resistance was at the base of CARP, where an Officer and a few men held out until the former was killed, when the remainder surrendered. For the rest the enemy, about 50 strong, fled from CARP before our second wave, who opened Lewis gun, rifle and grenade fire on them until the few who survived disappeared into our standing barrage.

About 40 of the enemy were accounted for in the first line, of which about 10 were taken prisoners; and a similar number were accounted for in the second line, where a few prisoners were also taken. In addition, the casualties caused by our standing barrage and our fire on those who retreated must have amounted to at least 100.

Many small dugouts were found to be occupied and bombed; the few men who made a show of resistance at the entrances being shot or bayonetted. The garrison was expecting relief by the 2/450th I.R. and their kits were packed up.

All dugouts were either blown up by the sappers or left in flames, in which case his stores of "pineapple" and "canister bombs" were thrown down the entrance. The 8 sappers who were attached to the raiding Companies did most excellent work.

Booby traps were made in CRAP, bombs with the pins removed being left under sandbags and dead bodies.

The tunnel under the GAVRELLE-FRESNES road could not be destroyed but men who debouched from it were bombed, and from a double block in the trench rifle grenades were fired into it point blank.

(2)

There was no trace of the suspected tunnel entrance in No Man's Land.

The enemy retaliation was slight; and allowed our party to return almost unmolested. Our withdrawal was perfectly timed in this respect. He fired seven 4.2" shells on to his front line about 4.45 p.m. but his guns did not get properly going until much later, when he heavily shelled GAVRELLE, WILLIE SUPPORT and our communication trenches, BELVOIR and TOWY ALLEY.

The loads carried were adequate and no material was brought back.

Five light machine guns and two pineapple-throwers were captured and brought back.

Communication throughout was excellent. The two wires which were taken forward from GRIGG trench held throughout, with the exception of one break which was repaired, and messages were sent to and forwarded immediately from Bn. Hqrs. in WILLIE SUPPORT in the pre-arranged code. At 4.37 p.m. the first message came through from GAVRELLE TRENCH.

The arrangements for the evacuation of wounded from both objectives to the Regimental Aid Post were very satisfactory; and the battalion Stretcher Bearers, with the volunteers who assisted them, worked with great zeal.

Our casualties were 1 Officer wounded, 2 other ranks killed and 19 wounded; with 3 exceptions all the wounds were slight and some of the men remained at duty. There were no casualties in the two garrison Companies during the night; these Companies reoccupied the front line after the raiding Companies had returned.

A wounded man who was brought in about 45 minutes after the raiders had returned reports that the enemy was putting out trip wire in front of his front line about 6 p.m.

Capt. G.A. BRETT was in command of the Raiders; with Capt. G.E. PALMER in command of C, the Right Company; and 2/Lieut. W.E. PHILLIPS in command of A, the Left Company.

B. THE GERMAN SYSTEM.

The wire was demolished and was no obstacle.

The front line is a ditch about 6 feet deep, with no fire-steps, revetments or trench gratings. The dugouts consist of about 6 steps down to a small chamber. There were some bomb and grenade dumps.

The second line is a better trench than the first, fully 6 feet deep and fire-stepped; but, like the first line, neither revetted nor trench-boarded.

Major,

G.S/A/2.
6.11.17.   Commanding, 1/23rd Bn. The London Regiment.

Army Form C. 2118.

WAR DIARY
or
INTELLIGENCE SUMMARY

(Erase heading not required.) 1/23rd.Battn.The London Regt.(T.F.)

Instructions regarding War Diaries and Intelligence Summaries are contained in F.S. Regs., Part II. and the Staff Manual respectively. Title Pages will be prepared in manuscript.

Place	Date	Hour	Summary of Events and Information	Remarks and references to Appendices
DECEMBER. 1917. Forward Area. 57.C:N.E. v	1.	6 a.m.	On relief Battn. proceeded to HUGHES SWITCH. H.Q. at K.10.a.5.5. (Sheet 57C.N.E.) 2 O.R. Wounded. 1 O.R. Missing.	
	2.	6 p.m.	Battn. moved to SUNKEN ROAD to relieve 1/6th.Battn.The Lon.Regt. and to support 1/8th.The Lon. Regt.who were to make an attack. Battn. in position 8 p.m. H.Q. at E.30.c.5.7., "A" Co. in SUNKEN ROAD E.24.b., "B" Co. on FONTAINE-BOURLON ROAD E.24.a., "C" & "D" Cos. SUNKEN ROAD at E.30.a.and c. (57.C:N.E.) 5.O.R. Killed. 13 O.R. Wounded.	
	3.	6 p.m.	Battn. moved to Front Line positions on left of BOURLON WOOD relieving 1/6th.,1/7th. & 1/8th. Battns.The Lon.Regt. H.Q. in old German gun pits at E.24.a.2.2. 1 O.R. Killed, 12 O.R. Wounded.	
	4.		Enemy shewed considerable activity all day.	
		3 p.m.	Four 5.9 guns near H.Q. blown up by R.E.s.	
		6 p.m.	Orders were received from 142nd.Inf.Bde. to evacuate positions and withdraw to HUGHES SWITCH Area. All S.A.A.,Bombs etc. from Battn.H.Q. and front line trenches collected and dumped on CAMBRAI-BAPAUME ROAD at E.24.c.5.4. to be salved. H.Q. moved back to HUGHES SWITCH at 11.45 p.m. 2/Lt.G.R.ALDRICH and 2 O.R. Killed.	
	5.	1 a.m.	The companies evacuated the front line by 1 a.m. and moved to new positions, leaving as rear-guard 2 platoons each of "B" & "C" Cos., and these withdrew at 4 a.m. "A" Co., "B" Co.(2 platoons) and "D" Co. occupied advanced posts at K.4.a.2.2., K.3.d.6.5. and K.4.d.1.5. respectively. "C" Co. and remainder of "B" Co. in HUGHES SWITCH. H.Q. at K.9.d.5.8. (57.C:N.E.)	
		8 a.m.	2 O.R.killed 4.O.R. Wounded.	
	6.. 7.. 8..		Heavy enemy shelling. 6 O.R.Killed. 20 O.R.Wounded.	

Lieut.Col.,
Cmdg. 1/23rd. Battn.London Regt.

Army Form C. 2118.

WAR DIARY
or
INTELLIGENCE SUMMARY

(Erase heading not required.)

1/23rd. Battn. The London Regt. (T.F.).

Instructions regarding War Diaries and Intelligence Summaries are contained in F.S. Regs., Part II and the Staff Manual respectively. Title Pages will be prepared in manuscript.

Place	Date	Hour	Summary of Events and Information	Remarks and references to Appendices
	DECEMBER 1917.			
57.C.N.E.	9.	7.30 a.m. to 11 a.m.	Enemy attacked "D" Co. Post, K.4.d.1.5., at 7.30 a.m. and succeeded in gaining a footing, but were almost immediately driven out with heavy loss. Enemy continued to show great signs of activity and the S.O.S. signal was fired continuosly for 1½ hours without response from our Artillery. The enemy attacked again at 11 a.m. and succeeded in penetrating between "D" Co. and left Co. of 1/21st.Lon.Regt. on the right. "D" Co. again repulsed the the attack but were compelled to shorten their frontage.	
		1 p.m.	At 1 p.m. the garrison withdrew to gun pits at K.4.c.5.2. All wounded casualties were cleared prior to evacuation, with the exception of 1 O.R. severely wounded. At dusk "D" Co. withdrew further to HUGHES SWITCH.	
		5 p.m.	Companies of the 1/22nd.Battn.Lon.Regt., attached to this Unit, were ordered to occupy defensive positions at K.3.d.7.2., K.4.e.5.1. and K.10.a.8.9. These posts were established by 10 p.m.	
		7 p.m.	and at 10.50 p.m. our "A" Co.& 2 platoons of "B" Co. evacuated their posts at K.4.a.2.2. and K.3.d.6.5. and withdrew to HUGHES SWITCH. 2/Lt.L.J.KENT-JONES Wounded, 2/Lt.W.E.PHILLIPS,M.C. Wounded at Duty. 13 O.R. Killed. 24 O.R. Wounded. 1 O.R. Wounded and Missing.	
	10.	9.30 a.m.	Considerable enemy shelling. 4 O.R. Wounded. Battn. Depot near NEUVILLE bombed by enemy aircraft at 9.30 a.m. Lt. and Q.M. C.A.JONES Wounded at Duty and 5 O.R. Wounded.	
	11.	8 p.m.	Battn. relieved by 1st.Battn.Royal Berks.Regt. and marched back to O.B.1. H.Q. in trench K.32.c.7.8. and the companies bivouaced at K.32.d.central approx.	
	12. to 15.		Battn. in reserve to 141st.Infantry Brigade.	
BERTINCOURT.	16.	Noon.	Battn. marched to billets at BERTINCOURT, bathing en route at RUYAULCOURT. Lt.W.G.SPENCER joined from the Base and posted to "D" Co.	
"	17.	7.30 a.m.	Battn. marched to VELU, entrained at 8.30 a.m. to AVELUY, and then proceeded by march route to billets at MILLENCOURT. (2.30 p.m.).	
MILLENCOURT.	18.	—	Companies at disposal of their respective commanders for general interior economy.	
"	19.	—	As previous day. Other Ranks paid in the afternoon.	

Signed Lieut.Col.,
Cmdg. 1/23rd.Battn. The London Regt.

WAR DIARY
or
INTELLIGENCE SUMMARY

(Erase heading not required.)

Army 1.

1/23rd.Battn.The London Regt.(T.F.)

Instructions regarding War Diaries and Intelligence Summaries are contained in F.S. Regs. Part II. and the Staff Manual respectively. Title Pages will be prepared in manuscript.

Place	Date	Hour	Summary of Events and Information	Remarks and references to Appendices
DECEMBER 1917.				
MILLENCOURT.	20.	9.30a.m.-12.30p.m.	Route marches under company arrangements. 1 N.C.O. per platoon received training under Divisional P.T.&B.F. Instructor. Lt.Col.A.MAXWELL,D.S.O. resumed command of the Battn. vice Major W.H.MURPHY to 1/18th.Lon.Regt. Lt.W.E.JONES and Lt.T.E.WEBSTER joined from the Base.	
"	21.	9.30a.m.-12.30p.m.	Route marches under company arrangements.	
"	22.	10a.m.-1p.m.	All Box Respirators tested by Divl. Gas N.C.O. Cos. carried out 2 hours training of Lewis Gunners. Other Ranks paid during afternoon.	
"	23.	9.30a.m.-11a.m. 10a.m.	Battn. allotted baths at SENLIS. Church Parade at 12 Noon. Billets inspected by Cmdg.Officer.	
"	24.	9-11a.m. 11-1p.m.	Gas Drill, Physical Training, General Musketry Instruction, & Specialist Training. Route marches under company arrangements.	
"	25.	10a.m.	Voluntary Holy Communion at HENNENCOURT.	
"	26.	9a.m.-1p.m.	Specialist and General Training. Company Route Marches.	
"	27.	9a.m.-1p.m. 10a.m.-3p.m.	"A" Co. fired on miniature range. Company training for "B","C",&"D"Cos. Specialist Training. Bde. Tactical Exercise for C.O.,2nd.in Command,& Adjt. I.O. with Signallers, Scouts& Runners.	
"	28.	9a.m.-1p.m.	"B" Co. fired on miniature range. Co. Training for A,C & D Cos. Specialist Training.	

[signature] Lt.,Col.,Cmdg.
1/23rd. Battn.The Lon.Regt.

Army Form C. 2118.

WAR DIARY
or
INTELLIGENCE SUMMARY

(Erase heading not required.)

1/23rd. Battn. The London Regt.(T.F.).

Place	Date	Hour	Summary of Events and Information	Remarks and references to Appendices
DECEMBER 1917.				
MILLENCOURT.	29.	9a.m.-1p.m.	"C" Co. on miniature range. Co.Training for A,B &D Cos. Specialist Training.	
"	30	11.30a.m. 7.p.m.	Church Parade. Previous to Parade C.O. inspected Billets. Battn.proceeded to Vth.Corps Area. Marched to ALBERT STATION & entrained to ETRICOURT.	
ETRICOURT.	31.	5 a.m.	Battn. detrained at ETRICOURT STATION and marched to Camp A3. nearby. on ROCQUIGNY ROAD.	
	1/1/1918.			

Cmdg. 1/23rd. Battn. The London Regiment.(T.F.).
Lieut.Col.",

Army Form C. 2118.

WAR DIARY
or
INTELLIGENCE SUMMARY

(Erase heading not required.)

1/23rd Bn The London Regt. T.F.

Vol 35

Place	Date	Hour	Summary of Events and Information	Remarks and references to Appendices
	January 1918.			
LECHELLE	1		Bn. rested in Camp.	
"	3	3 pm	" moved to HAVRINCOURT WOOD, Y Corps area.	
"	5		" Front line near RIBECOURT, relieving 9th Cheshire Regt. B left, C right front line; D left + A right support.	
RIBECOURT	7		Q.M. A.J. HARMAN took over command of "B" Coy vice Capt. G.C. PHILLIPS, to 3rd Army Musketry Camp.	
"	9		1 O.R. wounded. D relieved B, A Coy relieved "C". Considerable enemy artillery activity.	
"	10		2 O.R. killed.	
"	12		Bn. relieved by 8th Bn L.R. + moved by tram to billets at BERTINCOURT, arriving 5 pm 13/1/18.	
BERTINCOURT.	14		Interior economy. Awards of 1 D.S.O., 4 M.Cs and 14 M.Ms notified in connection with operations in December 1917. 3 Officers + 61 O.R. from Base.	
"	15		Physical drill, refitting &c	
"	16	9 am	Inspection of A + B Coys. Gas drill under Bn. Gas N.C.O.	

Jno. a. C. Sgt
Capt
Comdg 1/23rd Bn. London Regt

WAR DIARY or INTELLIGENCE SUMMARY

Army Form C. 2118.

1/23rd Bn The London Regt. T.F.

Place	Date	Hour	Summary of Events and Information	Remarks and references to Appendices
BERTINCOURT.	January 1918. 16		Lt W.G. SPENCER to command B Coy. vice Lt A.J. HARMAN, to D Coy. Pte D.G. LINTER killed by the collapse of a shelter, caused by the very high wind.	
"	17	11.30 am	Presentation of Medal ribbons by Major Gen. Sir F. GORRINGE, K.C.B., Comdg 47th (London) Div	
"	18		Bn. proceeded by train to TRESCAULT & relieved 20th Bn. L.R. in FLESQUIERES sector. B and C left, front line; A right, D left support.	
	21		A + D relieved B + C in front line.	
	23		Capt. G.A. BRETT, M.C. assumed command vice Major T.C. HARGREAVES, D.S.O., to leave.	
	24		Bn. relieved by 24th Bn. The London Regt. A, C + D to reserve in CHAPEL WOOD SWITCH. B Coy to TRESCAULT. Working Party of 50 O.R. hanging cable.	
	27		Lt G.W. CRISP to command B Coy vice Lt W.G. SPENCER, to leave.	
	28		Bn. (less A + D Coys) moved to support FLESQUIÈRES, relieving 21st Bn. L.R. who were transferred to 140 Inf. Bde. owing to reconstruction of Division. A + D in CHAPEL WOOD SWITCH. C on left. B on right.	
	31		Capt. G.A. BRETT, M.C., assumed command of Bn. vice Lt Col. A. MAXWELL, D.S.O., to leave. Temp. command of 140th. Inf. Bde.	

G.A. Brett Capt.
Commanding 1/23rd Bn. The London Regt.

Army Form C. 2118.

WAR DIARY
or
INTELLIGENCE SUMMARY
(Erase heading not required.)

1/23rd Battn The London Regt. T.F.

WA 36

Place	Date	Hour	Summary of Events and Information	Remarks and references to Appendices
	FEBRUARY, 1918.			
	2		Battn. relieved by 17th Battn. The London Regt. and marched to LONDON CAMP, near BERTINCOURT.	
LONDON CAMP	3		Battn. rested. 2/Lt P. BAMBROUGH reported for duty from 15th Bn London Regt.	
	4	9 am	Physical training (each Coy one hour) under Staff Instructor. Working party of 450 working on O.B.1. Battn. bathed at RUYAUCOURT.	
	5	9 a.m	Parades under Coy. arrangements.	
	6	9 am	Inspections, physical drill and drill under Coy. arrangements. Box Respirators inspected by Divl. Gas N.C.Os.	
		11 am	R.S.M's class for junior N.C.Os. Major A.T.FEARON, MC, assumed command of Battn.	
	7	9 am	Coy. drill, physical drill, etc. Working party of 30 under Town Major, RUYAULCOURT. Awards of two BELGIAN CROIX DE GUERRE announced (700010 RQMS E.Jones and 703880 Cpl N.R. SCUDAMORE, M.M.)	
	8		Bn entrained at BERTINCOURT, detrained at TRESCAULT and relieved 1/20th Bn London Regt. in RIBECOURT sector; B & C front line, A Support, D reserve.	
	9		Major T.C.HARGREAVES, DSO, from leave to England.	
	10		1 O.R. wounded. D and A Coys relieved B and C.	
	13		1 " " (since died of wounds)	

Army Form C. 2118.

WAR DIARY
or
INTELLIGENCE SUMMARY

(*Erase heading not required.*) 1/23rd Battn The London Regt. T.F.

Place	Date	Hour	Summary of Events and Information	Remarks and references to Appendices
	FEBRUARY, 1918.			
RIBECOURT	13		Capt D.J.Wardley, MC, from leave.	
	15		Capt E.M.Payne to leave; Capt D.J.WARDLEY, MC, resumed duties of Adjutant.	
	16		Bn relieved by 24th Bn London Regt. and moved into Reserve in RIBECOURT. 2/Lts. S. Holdsworth, W.G. Parish, F.J.C.Spurge and D. Ambrose from Base. 13 O.R. from Base.	
	19		Capt G.A.BRETT, MC, to leave.	
	22		Battn. relieved by DRAKE Battn. 63rd (R.N.) Division and moved to LONDON CAMP.	
	23	2.15pm	Bn paraded and marched to ROCQUIGNY area in "A" Camp.	
ROCQUIGNY	24	10.15 am	Church Parade.	
	25		Refitting, cleaning of arms, equipment, &c.	
	26		8 a.m: to 6 p.m. Battn. bathed at ROCQUIGNY Baths. Major T.C. HARGREAVES, DSO, assumed command of Battn. vice Major A.T.FEARON, MC.	
	27.	8 am	Each Coy. one hour on range. Coy. drill, physical drill, etc.	
	28		Battn. marched to GUEDUECOURT area and carried out Field Firing. Dinners in the field. 13 O.R. from Reinforcement Camp.	

G.N.Hargreaves Major,

Commanding, 1/23rd Battn. The London Regiment.

1/23RD BATTALION,
THE LONDON
REGIMENT.

No. 3. 18.
Date...........

47th Division.
142nd Infantry Brigade.

WAR DIARY

1/23rd BATTALION

LONDON REGIMENT

MARCH 1918

Army Form C. 2118.

WAR DIARY
or
INTELLIGENCE SUMMARY

(Erase heading not required.)

O.C. 1/23rd Bn. The London Regt. T.F.

Instructions regarding War Diaries and Intelligence Summaries are contained in F. S. Regs., Part II. and the Staff Manual respectively. Title Pages will be prepared in manuscript.

Place	Date March 1918	Hour	Summary of Events and Information	Remarks and references to Appendices
BUSCOURT	1	9 am	Bn. Parade and drill. Firing on 100 and 50 yd. range.	
	2	9 am	" Platoon training until 1.30 pm	
	3	9.30 am	Parade Service. C.O. inspected Camp. 42 O.R. from Base.	
	4–6		Bn. and Coy. training.	
	7	8.30 am	Bn. marched to DAILLY SAILLISEL area for attack practice. U. Col. MAXWELL, D.S.O., T.D. resumed command of Bn.	
	8	9.45 am	Brigade tactical exercise ('D' Coy represented the enemy)	
	9		A & B and C & D practised attack in pairs. Musketry + gas drill	
	10		Parade Service. Summer time came into use as from 11 pm. 12 O.R. from Base.	
	11	11 am	Bn. the inspected by G.O.C. 142nd Inf. Bde. Coy. training. A Coy. under Capt. AW DURRANT D.S.O., found working party on Corps Defence line. B Coy. carried out Coy. Training	
	13	9 am	Bn. carried out Tactical exercise near Camp. 5 O.R. from Base.	
	14		Bn. under Major T.C. HARGREAVES, D.S.O., working party for C.R.E. 2nd Division.	
	15		BCoD " Capt. BA BRETT, M.C. " 47th Division.	
		11 am	1 pm "A" carried out Coy. training.	
	16	8	150 O.R. from A & B Coys. under Capt. W.G. SPENCER, working in forward area	
		8	CoD Inspections + Platoon training.	

WAR DIARY
or
INTELLIGENCE SUMMARY

(Erase heading not required.)

O / Warren Bell
O.C. 1/23rd Bn. The London Regt. T.F.

Instructions regarding War Diaries and Intelligence Summaries are contained in F. S. Regs., Part II. and the Staff Manual respectively. Title Pages will be prepared in manuscript.

Place	Date	Hour	Summary of Events and Information	Remarks and references to Appendices
ROCQUIGNY	March 1918 17	8 am	Working Party of 100 OR. (C+D) under 2/Lt W.E. JONES	
	18	10.15	Parade Service. 11 OR transferred to 117th Bn. M.G.C.	
	19	8.30 am	Training under Coy. arrangements. Inspections, refitting &c. S/Lt C.W. WALKER, sick to Hospital. 2/Lt J.G GARTHWAITE from Hosp. 9 OR. from Base. During above period special classes for training Signallers, Lewis Gunners and Bombers were held and a good deal of musketry was carried out, including competitions for Regimental Cups.	
	20		Bn. marched to METZ in Divisional Reserve. Depôt moved to EQUANCOURT.	
	21	4.20 am	Enemy opened terrific bombardment. A, B + C occupied METZ Switch. H.Q and D Coy in METZ. 2/Lt W.E PHILLIPS, M.C., wounded. 3 Lieut. of "A" Coy killed. Capt G.A BRETT, M.C., + Capt E.M. PAYNE /c Forward Battn. H.Q.	
	22	8 pm	A, B + C moved forward to form a defensive flank along line NEW SWITCH stretching from N of GOUZECOURT WOOD to Winchester Valley, to cover retirement of troops from 2nd system. In position at 9 pm. 2 Platoons of D Coy moved forward to Forward Bn. HQ. Depôt moved to BUS.	
	23	3 AM	A, B + C withdrew from NEW SWITCH + occupied portion of METZ SWITCH, S. of Winchester Valley, this becoming Brittal front line. "B" right, "A" left, "C" support. Bn ordered to hold METZ SWITCH until ordered to withdraw. At daybreak (5.30 am) German attack developed from GOUZECOURT Ridge. Repeated attacks from enemy advanced troops were	

WAR DIARY
or
INTELLIGENCE SUMMARY
(Erase heading not required.)

Instructions regarding War Diaries and Intelligence Summaries are contained in F.S. Regs. Part II. and the Staff Manual respectively. Title Pages will be prepared in manuscript.

O/C fireman left to 23rd instr Ryf

Place	Date	Hour	Summary of Events and Information	Remarks and references to Appendices
BATTLE ZONE	23rd (contd)	10.30	repulsed by rifle and L.G. fire. 2/Lt CF WOOLHOUSE wd. Orders received to hold position until 1.30 p.m. — withdrawal commenced 30 minutes before ZERO in order, A, B, C. Withdrawal covered by Reef Coy 'D' Coy, which had lined the outskirts of METZ. Bn. moved under heavy M.G. and shell fire to position NE of EQUANCOURT, arriving at about 2 p.m. Owing to heavy M.G. fire from right flank, position soon became untenable & withdrawal was continued in direction of VALHUART WOOD. Bn. billeted at DEVONSHIRE CAMP, W. of ROCQUIGNY for night. Dept moved to front on BAPAUME – PERONNE road near LE TRANSLOY.	ZERO = 30
	24	8 a.m.	Bn. occupied defensive line along sunken road running S.W. from LE TRANSLOY.	
		3 p.m.	" moved to trenches near GUEUDECOURT, leaving these later for HIGH WOOD, arriving at dusk, where extant line was occupied W. of the wood. Owing to the impossibility of locating this position after daybreak, at 2.30 a.m. (25th) Bn. withdrew through BAZENTIN-LE-PETIT to CONTALMAISON	
	25	6 a.m.	Bn. took up defensive position on left of Divl. front on high ground between CONTALMAISON and BAZENTIN-LE-PETIT.	
		10.30 a.m.	Bn. moved forward 1,000 yards & occupied road on ridge 650 yds. W. of BAZENTIN-WOOD in support. Dept moved from LES BOEUFS at 10 a.m. 24th (being shelled out) and moved to CONTALMAISON which here the Brigade transport was bombed by several enemy aeroplanes, but suffered	

WAR DIARY
or
INTELLIGENCE SUMMARY

(Erase heading not required.)

1/23rd Bn The London Regt.

Place	Date	Hour	Summary of Events and Information	Remarks and references to Appendices
BATTLE ZONE	March 1918		no casualties. Dept moved. Bn on left of ALBERT-MILLEN COURT road; about 10.30 pm bombs were dropped very near to camping ground but no damage was done.	
	25		Depôt moved to field near MILLEN COURT.	
	26.	1 am	Owing to the defection of Battn on left, the Battn. was forced to withdraw to LA BOISELLE Ridge and, on relief by 12th Division, withdraw to SENLIS for reorganisation. Depôt moved to SENLIS.	
		4 pm		
	27	9 am	Bn. marched to billets at VAUCHELLE.	
	28	1.30 am	"" moved to defensive outpost line E. of HARPONVILLE. Depôt moved to TOUTENCOURT. Capt A.J. HARMAN M.C. i/c command of Bath. "" "" Hicks at WARLOY. Estimated Casualties period 21–26th:– Killed : 1 Officer, 19 O.R. Wounded : 8 Officers, 94 O.R. Missing : 8 Officers, 141 O.R.	
	29–	10 pm	Batt. moved into support in MARTINSART village.	
	30.		MARTINSART.	
	31.		2/Lt. A.G. KIRK killed.	

142nd Brigade.
47th Division.

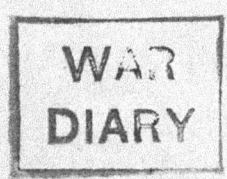

1/23rd BATTALION

THE LONDON REGIMENT.

APRIL 1 9 1 8

Report on Operations at AVELUY WOOD 5th & 6th April.

Army Form C. 2118.

WAR DIARY or INTELLIGENCE SUMMARY

(Erase heading not required.)

Vol 38

22nd Bn. Lon. Regt.

Place	Date APRIL, 1918	Hour	Summary of Events and Information	Remarks and references to Appendices
MARTINSART.	1		Battn. in trenches.	
	4	p.m.	Battn. relieved 22nd Battn. C & D front line, A & B support.	
AVELUY WOOD 57 D 1/20,000	5	6 a.m	Enemy started to shell our front line until 8.30 a.m. when he advanced in small groups against "C" Coy. (2/Lt W.G.IRWIN) but were repulsed by L.G. fire. At 9.20 a.m. A Coy. went forward to reinforce "C" Coy. At 9.25 a.m. S.O.S. went up along entire Battn. front. At 10.30 a.m. "C" Coy's right flank was forced back - left flank was in the WOOD. "D" Coy, on left of front line attacked by overwhelming numbers and surrounded. Survivors state that the Coy. met the enemy with rifles and Lewis guns but were unable to prevent him getting in their rear. Lieut. H.S. EWEN, M.O., 2/Lt G.H.CRISP and 2/Lt W.J.KEMP Missing; 2/Lt C.J. STRICKLAND killed in action. At 11.30 a.m. enemy had penetrated between our front Companies. Owing to heavy M.G. fire from left rear, A & C Coys. were forced back to communication trench running from WOOD to Battn. H.Q. and established communication with 24th Bn. London Regt. on left along the edge of the WOOD. (11.40 a.m.)	
		p.m. 12.30	Major R.H.TOLERTON, M.G. (temporarily commanding Battn.) went to MARTINSART to arrange counter-attack with 22nd Bn. About 12.40 p.m. A & C Coys. suffered heavy casualties from enfilade M.G. fire from direction of W.10. central.	
		p.m. 4.15	Two Coys. 22nd Battn. attacked AVELUY WOOD to re-establish original line. The Battn. covered the attack with rifle and L.G. fire. Owing to heavy M.G. fire from edge of WOOD and absence of artillery support, the counter-attack failed. Major TOLERTON wounded in head. Capt. COOK, 22nd Bn., assumed command of troops of 22nd and 23rd Battns., who fell back on line of C.T. and bank.	
		p.m. 11	Battn. strength - 5 Officers, 150 O.R.	
	6		Battn. heavily shelled all day. About 6.30 p.m. small parties of the enemy left the WOOD opposite our Right Coy. and ran in S. direction. They were caught in our L.G. fire.	
	7	a.m. 2.45	Relief of Battn. by 17th Royal Scots completed. Battn. returned to billets at WARLOY.	

Army Form C. 2118.

WAR DIARY
or
INTELLIGENCE SUMMARY

(Erase heading not required.)   1/23rd Bn. The London Regt.

Instructions regarding War Diaries and Intelligence Summaries are contained in F.S. Regs., Part II. and the Staff Manual respectively. Title Pages will be prepared in manuscript.

Place	Date	Hour	Summary of Events and Information	Remarks and references to Appendices
WARLOY.	8		Battn. marched to billets at RAINCHEVAL. Draft of 156 O.R. from Base.	
RAINCHEVAL	9		Refitting and reorganisation.	
	10		Battn. marched to billets at MONTRELET.	
MONTRELET	11		" " " " YVRENCHEUX.	
YVRENCHEUX	12		Battn. rested and reorganised.	
	13		Reorganisation. All Lewis gunners classified.	
	14	11.30 a.m.	Divine Service. Commanding Officer inspected billets. 32 O.R. from Base.	
	15		Coy. and Specialist Training, including Physical drill and musketry on ranges. 9 o.r. from Base.	
	16		Coy. Training and firing on range. Box respirators inspected by Divl. Gas N.C.Os.	
	17		Coy. and Specialist training.	
	18	9.50 a.m.	Battalion tactical exercise.	
	19	8.30 10 a.m.	Coy. Training and musketry. Companies carried out practice attack.	
	20	8.30 10.30	Coy. Training, &c. Battn. Tactical Exercise.	
	21	10.	Divine Service. Commanding Officer inspected billets.	
	22	8.30 12.30	Physical drill, musketry, firing on range. Details firing on Range. Divl. Commander (Major General Sir G.F.GORRINGE) addressed 23rd and 24th Battns, on recent operations.	

2449 Wt. W14957/M90 750,000 1/16 J.B.C. & A. Forms/C.2118/12.

Army Form C. 2118.

WAR DIARY
or
INTELLIGENCE SUMMARY
(Erase heading not required.)

Place	Date	Hour	Summary of Events and Information	Remarks and references to Appendices
YVRENCHEUX	APRIL, 1918.			
	23	8.30	Physical drill, musketry, etc., under Coy. arrangements.	
		10.30	Coys. practised adoption of defensive positions, working in pairs.	
		p.m. 2.30	Lewis Gunners on Range. 6 Officers, 6 O.R. from Base.	
	24	8.30	Physical drill, musketry and firing on range.	
		11	Battn. practised taking up a defensive position, against which "C" delivered an attack. Battalion SPORTS MEETING. 12 Officers, 12 O.R. from Base.	
	25	8.30	Musketry, firing on range, etc. under Coy. arrangements.	
	26	11	Battn. Attack Practice. 1 Officer, 96 Other Ranks from Base. 150 O.R. from 15th Bn London Regt. attached. Training under Coy. arrangements.	
	27	[?] 11	Musketry on Range. Battn. paraded and marched to billets at MARCHEVILLE, practising advanced rear guards on road. 6 O.R.	
	28	10.15	Battn. attended special Parade Service held by Deputy Chaplain General near BRAILLY. presented with decorations won in recent operations.	
	29	9 a.m.	Battn. embussed at FROYELLES and proceeded to WARLOY and billeted.	
	30		Battn. rested; usual refitting, etc., before proceeding to the Line.	
2nd May 1918.				

Lieut. Colonel,
Commanding, 1/23rd Battn. The London Regiment.

Sheet 57d
1/20,000.

Report on the Operations at AVELUY WOOD on 5th and 6th, April 1918.

23rd Bn relieved 22nd Bn. night 4/5th April 1918; night was quiet.

5th April 1918.

6 a.m.	Enemy started to shell our front line. His barrage started North of our position and crept gradually South. Heavy bombardment of valley S. of MARTINSART. Shelling continued with increasing intensity till
8 a.m.	S.O.S. sent up from Battn. H.Q. Enemy fired a number of gas shells near Battn. H.Q.
8.30 a.m.	C Coy. (right front) reported enemy advanced in small groups against their front, but were repulsed by L.G. fire.
8.35 a.m.	All wires from Bn. H.Q. disconnected. Message re situation sent to Brigade per runner.
9.20 a.m.	A Coy (right support) ordered forward to reinforce C Coy - Brigade informed via 22nd Battn.
9.25 a.m.	S.O.S. seen along entire Battn. front. Signal repeated at Battn. H.Q.
10.30 a.m.	C Coy's right flank forced back - left flank in WOOD. D Coy. (left front) attacked by overwhelming numbers and surrounded. Survivors state Company met enemy with rifles and Lewis guns but were unable to prevent him getting in their rear. Our artillery (4.5's) dropped short on edge of WOOD, causing several casualties. Brigade informed.
11.30 a.m.	Capt. A.J.HARMAN, M.C., went to H.Q., 24th Battn. to establish communication with our right flank. Report sent to Brigade that enemy had penetrated between our front Companies and established three M.G. posts about W.4.a.4.5.
11.40 a.m.	Owing to heavy M.G. fire from left rear, A & C Coys. were forced back to communication trench running from WOOD to Battn. H.Q. They established connection with 24th Bn. on left along edge of Wood.
12.30 p.m.	Major R.H.TOLERTON, M.C., left Battn. H.Q. to arrange counter attack, which 22nd Bn - in MARTINSART - had been ordered to make.
12.40 p.m.	Enemy reported massing South of AVELUY WOOD - about W.10.a.4.8. M.G. Coy. requested to train two guns along edge of WOOD in front of our A & B Coys. (W.4.c.3.4 to W.10.a.3.6). Request complied with. A Coy. in touch with M.G.Coy. on right. About this period heavy casualties were caused to A & C Coys. (in communication trench and along bank) by enfilade M.G. fire from direction of Nissen Hut Camp about W.10. central.
1.30 p.m.	Message picked up from 20th Battn. power buzzer "Enemy reported moving forward from Wood in W.4.b." Repeated to 24th Battn - who acknowledged and stated they had no further news re our "D" Coy.
3.30 p.m.	Major R.H.TOLERTON, M.C., returned from H.Q., 22nd Bn. ZERO for counter attack fixed for 4 p.m.
3.50 p.m.	ZERO advanced to 4.15 p.m. 22nd Bn. informed.

(2)

4.15 p.m.   Two Companies 22nd Bn. attacked AVELUY WOOD with the
            intention of re-establishing original line. 23rd Bn.
            covered attack with rifle and L.G. fire. Owing to
            heavy M.G. fire from edge of WOOD and absence of any
            artillery support, counter attack failed.
            Major R.H.TOLERTON, M.C., wounded in head; after
            dressing he left for 142 Inf Bde H.Q.
            Capt. COOK assumed command of troops of 22nd and 23rd
            Bns., who fell back on line of C.T. and bank.

6.5 p.m.   Message sent to Brigade confirming failure of counter
            attack. Touch established with 20th and 24th Bns.
            Former in touch on right with BUFFS.

10.20 p.m. Request to 24th Bn. that they should lay a wire from
            their H.Q. to ours. Request was complied with. This
            line held until we were relieved.

10.30 p.m. Fighting patrol of 2/Lt MAYES and 10 O.R. of 22nd Bn.
            worked along Battn. front. Enemy quiet.

11 p.m.   Battn. strength - 5 Officers, 150 O.R.
            Night quiet.

6th April 1918.

1.20 a.m.   Slight hostile gas shelling of area.

1.30 a.m.   Major MARSHALL, 4th R.W.F., arrived at joint Bn H.Q.

2.30 a.m.   Fighting patrol under Lieut. RICHARDS covered our front
            but did not come into contact with the enemy.

5.30 a.m.   Counter-attacking troops of 4th R.W.F. in position.

5.55 a.m.   Counter attack by 4th R.W.F. launched under cover of
            creeping barrage; repulsed with heavy casualties owing
            to failure of barrage to silence hostile M.Gs. On
            left, small party of R.W.F. succeeded in establishing
            a post on edge of WOOD to right of head of C.T.
            20th and 24th Bns. informed as to situation.

6.10 a.m.   Message sent direct by runner to 77th Brigade R.F.A.
            giving situation of our line and asking for shoot on
            S.W. corner of WOOD.

            Situation normal during morning. Enemy shelled MARTIN-
            SART heavily during day.

4 p.m.   C.O. 17th Royal Scots arrived to reconnoitre

6.10 p.m.   Brigade warned us that enemy had been seen massing in
            S.E. corner of WOOD.

6.30 p.m.   Enemy commenced heavy bombardment of our right front
            and of the valley S. of AVELUY WOOD. As shelling
            grew intense, S.O.S. signal was fired and Stokes
            Mortars opened fire on Southern edge of WOOD.
            Enemy shelled along valley between MARTINSART and WOOD
            but did not shell our front line. MARTINSART heavily
            shelled.
            During the bombardment, which continued intensely, small
            parties of enemy left edge of WOOD opposite our right
            Coy. and ran in S. direction. They were caught in our
            L.G. fire.
            Arrangements were made to form a defensive flank on right
            - whence enemy threat appeared to come. Runners were
            sent back to H.Q. 22nd Bn. asking reserve Coy. to hold
            itself in readiness for this purpose.

About 8 p.m. shelling died down and situation was normal during remainder of night.

7th April 1918.

2.45 a.m.   Relief of 23rd Battn. by 17th Royal Scots completed.

                                                                       Lieut. Colonel,

Comdg., 1/23rd Bn. The London Regiment.

Army Form C. 2118.

WAR DIARY
or
INTELLIGENCE SUMMARY

(Erase heading not required.)   1/23rd Bn The London Regt. T.F.

Instructions regarding War Diaries and Intelligence Summaries are contained in F. S. Regs., Part II. and the Staff Manual respectively. Title Pages will be prepared in manuscript.

VE 39

Place	Date	Hour	Summary of Events and Information	Remarks and references to Appendices
MAY, 1918.				
WARLOY.	1		Battn. relieved 20th Battn. A.I.F. in left subsector, HENENCOURT. A right front, B left, C Support, D reserve. H.Q. W.20.a.1.9. (57D). Major R.H.TOLERTON, M.C., rejoined from Hospital and apptd. Second-in-Command of Battn. This Officer took over command of Battn. in line.	
	4		Heavy shelling on 3rd and 4th. 2 O.R. wounded.	
	5		C & D relieved A & B respectively in front line.	
	9	A.M. 3.30	Enemy placed a heavy barrage on our front and support lines, together with considerable rifle and M.G. fire. At 3.35 a.m. there was a lull, and no rifle, etc., fire was heard. At 3.40 a.m. the enemy barrage intensified and at 3.55 a.m. the enemy attacked and drove part of our left front coy ("D") from the trench for about 150 yards. At 4 a.m. the enemy in our front line fired green lights. Two immediate counter-attacks (the first shortly after 4 a.m. by Nos 14 and 15 platoons, the second at about 7 a.m. by 2 platoons of "A" Coy.) were unsuccessful. At 11 p.m. Nos 6, 7 & 8 platoons successfully counter-attacked. 3 Germans (1 officer, 1 W.O. and 1 man), 2 light machine guns were captured, and a Lewis gun re-captured. Casualties for the day: Lieuts. J.D.L. REID and G.M. REID killed, 13 O.R. killed, 2/Lts. W.W. CARRUTHERS, J.D. FLYNN and Lt W.G. MOORE and 44 O.R. wounded. 5 O.R. missing.	Estimated German casualties 90, of whom 40 were killed.
	10		Bn relieved by 18th Bn London Regt. and returned to billets at WARLOY-BAILLON.	
WARLOY.	11	11.15 12 noon	Parade service. Baths at WARLOY. Reorganisation and refitting of Companies.	
	13	9 a.m.	Platoon and physical drill, musketry exercises, Specialist training.	
	14		Working party of 250 O.R. (A, B & C Coys under Capt G.C.PHILLIPS) digging trench for cable.	
	15		" " " " " (B, C, & D) - do -) " " "	
	16		Bn relieved 11 Bn R.F. (18th Division) in Corps Reserve in BAZIEUX system.	

Army Form C. 2118.

WAR DIARY
or
INTELLIGENCE SUMMARY

(Erase heading not required.) 1/23rd Bn The London Regt.

Instructions regarding War Diaries and Intelligence Summaries are contained in F.S. Regs., Part II. and the Staff Manual respectively. Title Pages will be prepared in manuscript.

Place	Date	Hour	Summary of Events and Information	Remarks and references to Appendices
	MAY, 1918.			
	18		28 O.R. joined from 17th Bn London Regt.	
	19		21 " " " " " " " "	
	23		5 " " " " " " " (16 O.R. still at Divl. Wing).	
	21		Lt H.H.HENTHORNE and 4 O.R. joined Div. Wing from Base.	
	22		1 O.R. killed by enemy bomb during night at BAIZIEUX.	
	24		2/Lt R.A. TOMLIN and 9 O.R. joined Divl. Wing from Base.	
			During the above period the Battalion worked on improving the BAIZIEUX system.	
	24		Battn. relieved 11 Bn R.F. in support in front of BRESLE, near ALBERT.	
	25		2/Lt L.G. ATKINS and 3 O.R. killed, 7 O.R. wounded.	
	26		2/Lt R. HICKS and 3 O.R. killed, 5 O.R. wounded.	
	27		1 O.R. wounded. Lt & Q.M. C.A.JONES, special leave to U.K.	
	28		2/Lts S.R.W. WALKER, R.P. GOLDSMITH, S. VAUGHAN and F.H.STARR taken on strength (joined Wing 21/5/18).	
	29		1 O.R. wounded, 1 O.R. accidentally wounded.	
	31		Lt Col A.MAXWELL, DSO, TD, proceeded on short leave to U.K. (2 - 14/6/18). Major R.H. TOLERTON, M.C., assumed command of Battalion.	
	2/6/18.			

(signature) Major,
Commanding, 1/23rd Battn. The London Regt.

Army Form C. 2118.

WAR DIARY
or
INTELLIGENCE SUMMARY

(Erase heading not required.)

Instructions regarding War Diaries and Intelligence Summaries are contained in F.S. Regs., Part II. and the Staff Manual respectively. Title Pages will be prepared in manuscript.

23rd Bn. Lon Regt

Vol 40

Place	Date	Hour	Summary of Events and Information	Remarks and references to Appendices
BRESLE. LAVIEVILLE.	JUNE 1st.	11.30p.m.	Battalion in Support. Battn relieved by 1/21st Battn The London Regt and marched to position in LAVIEVILLE Trench System. H.Q. at D.9.b.5.8 (62 D).	
LAHOUSSOYE	5th	M'night.	Battn relieved by 1/22nd Battn The London Regt and marched to position in the LAHOUSSOYE Trench System O.21.B (62D)	
	8th		T/Lt A.A.R.D.le POER-POWER (A.S.C.) and 2/Lt C.B.C.M.LEDGERTON(17th London) joined 47 Div'l Reception Camp from Base.	
LEFT SUB-SECTOR.	9th	M'night.	Battn relieved 1/19th Battn The London Regt in Left Subsector, ALBERT. "C" Coy Right Front "A" Coy Left Front, "B" Coy in Support, "D" Coy in Reserve. H.Q. at D.12.d.6.6. (62D). Capt H.C.D.Miller RAMC relieved by 1/Lt. H.W.M.Robertson, MORC USA.	
	10th		Capt E.M.Payne, MC, Lieut S.A.Gray, 2/Lt S.Vaughan, 2/Lt R.P.Goldsmith and 2/Lt S.R.W. Walker joined Battn from Div'l Reception Camp.	
	12th		2 O.R. Wounded	
	13th		B Coy relieved C Coy in Right Front, D Coy relieved A Coy in Left Front. Capt A.J.Harman, MC & 2/Lt J.H.Hornby Wounded & returned to duty after A.T.S. injection. 2 O.R. Wounded.	
	14th		1 O.R. Killed in Action.	
	15th		3 O.R. Killed in Action. 4 O.R. Wounded.	
	16th		3 O.R. Killed in Action.	
	17th		4 O.R. Killed in Action.	
	18th		Lt Col A.MAXWELL, DSO, TD rejoined from short leave to U.K.	
	19th		2 O.R. Wounded.	

Major,
Comdg 1/23rd Battn The London Regt.

Army Form C. 2118.

WAR DIARY
or
INTELLIGENCE SUMMARY

(Erase heading not required.)

Instructions regarding War Diaries and Intelligence Summaries are contained in F. S. Regs., Part II. and the Staff Manual respectively. Title Pages will be prepared in manuscript.

1/23rd Bn [?]

Place	Date	Hour	Summary of Events and Information	Remarks and references to Appendices
LEFT SUBSECTOR ALBERT.	JUNE. 19th	M'night	Battn relieved by 2/2nd Battn The London Regt and marched to billets at BEHENCOURT, arriving 3.30 a.m. H'qrs in CHATEAU.	
BEHENCOURT	20th		Battn resting & refitting. Lieut H.H.Henthorne, Lieut.A.A.R.D.le Poer-Power, 2/Lt C.B.C.M. Ledgerton, 2/Lt L.F.Fisher, 2/Lt F.H.Starr, 2/Lt W.G.Irwin & 2/Lt G.F.Taylor joined Battn from Div'l Reception Camp.	
	21st	8 p.m.	Battn moved by bus to BOUGAINVILLE via AMIENS -G.H.Q.Reserve.	
BOUGAINVILLE	22nd		Coys at disposal of Coy Commanders for interior economy etc.	
	23rd	10 a.m.	Church Parade. Billets inspected by Commanding Officer.	
	24th	8.30 a.m.- 12.30 p.m.	Battn, Company & Platoon Drill on Training Ground at O.9.d.(Sheet 62 E) Signallers carried out 4 hours' training under O.C.Sigs.	
		10.30 a.m. - 12.30 p.m.	"A" Coy Firing & musketry exercises on Range.	
		2.30 p.m.	Junior N.C.O.s under R.S.M.	
		6 p.m.	Lecture by Lt Col A.Maxwell, DSO to all Officers "Lessons to be derived from the recent fighting".	
	25th	8.30 a.m.-12.30 p.m.	Battn Company & Platoon training. 1½ hours' specialists training. Sigs as on 24th. B Coy on Range.	
		6 p.m.	Lecture by Lt Col A.Maxwell DSO to N.C.O.s - subject as on 24th.	
	26th	8.30 a.m.-12.30 p.m.	Training as on 25th. C Coy on Range.	
	27th	8.30 a.m.-12.30 p.m.	Training as on previous day. D Coy on Range.	
		2.30 p.m.	N.C.Os & No 1 of Lewis Gun teams instructed in use of BARR & STROUD Range-finder.	
		6 p.m.	Lecture by Major R.H.Tolerton, MC to Officers & Sergts.	
		9.30-10.30 p.m.	A Coy practised Scouting & Patrolling by platoons.	

Cmdg 1/23rd Battn The London Regt.

[signature], Major,

Army Form C. 2118.

WAR DIARY
or
INTELLIGENCE SUMMARY

(Erase heading not required.)

Instructions regarding War Diaries and Intelligence Summaries are contained in F. S. Regs., Part II. and the Staff Manual respectively. Title Pages will be prepared in manuscript.

Place	Date	Hour	Summary of Events and Information	Remarks and references to Appendices
BOUGAINVILLE.	JUNE 28th	8.30a.m.-12.30p.m.	Training as previous days. H.Qrs Details on Range.	
		6 p.m.	Riding Class for Officers under Major R.H.Tolerton,MC	
		9.30-10.30p.m.	B Coy exercised in Scouting & Patrolling by platoons.	
		6 p.m.	Inoculation of O.R. who had not been inoculated during the last 12 months.	
	29th	8.30 a.m.-12.30 p.m.	Training as previous days. B Coy Lewis Gunners on Range under L.G.O. Cash payments to troops.	
	30th	10 a.m.	Church Parade. Billets inspected by Commanding Officer.	
		2-7.30 p.m.	Battalion Sports Meeting.	

Robert Oakey Major.
Comdg 1/23rd Battn The London Regiment. T.F. 2/7/1918.

Army Form C. 2118.

1/23rd Lon.Regt.   • WAR DIARY •
JULY 1918.   or
                INTELLIGENCE SUMMARY
                (Erase heading not required.)

Instructions regarding War Diaries and Intelligence
Summaries are contained in F. S. Regs., Part II.
and the Staff Manual respectively. Title Pages
will be prepared in manuscript.

1/23rd Lon.Regt.   Vol 4/1

Place	Date	Hour	Summary of Events and Information	Remarks and references to Appendices
BOUGAINVILLE.	JULY 1st.		Major R.H.Tolerton, M.C. assumed command of Battalion vice Lt Col A. Maxwell, DSO, TD, appointed G.O.C. 174th Inf Bde.	
		8.30 a.m. – 12.30 p.m.	Company and Specialist Training. Battn Ceremonial Drill.	
	2nd	8.30 a.m. – 12.30 p.m.	Training as on previous day.	
		10.30 a.m. – 12.30 p.m.	C Coy Lewis Gunners on Range.	
		2.30 p.m. – 4 p.m.	8 men per platoon A Coy attended lecture & demonstration on No. 36 Grenade.	
		2.30 p.m. – 4 p.m.	Tactical Scheme practised by Coy Commanders. Discussion thereon at H.Qrs at 6 p.m.	
	3rd	8.30 a.m. – 12.30 p.m.	Training as on previous days.	
		9 a.m. – 10 a.m.	A and B Coys bathed in the lake at OISSY CHATEAU.	
		10.30 a.m.– 12.30 p.m.	D Coy Lewis Gunners on Range.	
		2.30 p.m. – 4 p.m.	Junior N.C.O.s drilled under R.S.M.	
	4th	7 a.m.	Battalion embussed to Rifle Range near AMIENS in R.1 & R.2 (Sheet 62E). Range and Field Firing carried out. Battn returned to billets at 6 p.m.	
	5th	8.30 a.m. – 12.30 p.m.	Battalion Drill. Coy and Platoon training in the attack. Specialist Training.	
		2.30 p.m. – 4 p.m.	8 men per platoon B Coy attended lecture & demonstration on No. 36 Grenade.	
		9.30 p.m. – 10.30 p.m.	C Coy carried out scouting and patrolling exercises by platoons under their own officers.	
	6th	8.30 a.m. – 12.30 p.m.	Training as on previous day.	
			Afternoon devoted to Interior Economy – Cash payments to the Troops.	
	7th	10 a.m.	Church Parade followed by inspection of billets by Commanding Officer.	
		2 p.m.	Battn marched to OISSY to attend 142 Inf Bde Gymkhana in Chateau grounds.	
	8th	8.30 a.m. – 12.30 p.m.	Training as on the 6th July.	
		2.30 p.m. – 4 p.m.	8 men per platoon C Coy attended lecture & demonstration on No. 36 Grenade.	
	9th (next sheet)			

Robert Tolerton Major,
Comdg., 1/23rd Battn The London Regiment. (T.F.)

2/8/18.

Army Form C. 2118.

WAR DIARY
INTELLIGENCE SUMMARY
(Erase heading not required.)

Place	Date	Hour	Summary of Events and Information	Remarks and references to Appendices
BOUGAINVILLE.	JULY. 9th	8.30 a.m. – 12.30 p.m. 2.30 p.m. – 4 p.m.	Training as on previous days. 8 men per platoon D Coy attended lecture and demonstration on No. 36 Grenade. Battn won 142 Inf Bde Transport Competition at OISSY CHATEAU.	
	10th	8.30 a.m. – 12.30 p.m. 10.30 a.m. – 12.30 p.m.	Training as on previous days. Lewis Gunners (not considered proficient) on Range.	
	11th	8.30 a.m. – 12.30 p.m. 6.30 p.m.	Training as on previous days. Battalion Church Parade.	
	12th	10 a.m.	Battn marched to near BRIQUEMESNIL & embussed at noon to WARLOY-BAILLON, debussing at 4.30 p.m.	
FORWARD AREA. "		11 p.m.	Battn relieved 7th BUFFS in front line. H.Qrs at W.19.b.6.4. (Sheet 57 D) A Coy... Left Front Coy. C Coy... Right Front Coy. D Coy... Support Coy. B Coy... Reserve Coy.	
	13th		1 O.R. Killed-in-Action : 3 O.R. Wounded : 1 O.R. Wounded (S.I.W.)	
	15th		1 O.R. Wounded.	
	16th		5 O.R. Wounded.	
	17th		2 O.R. Wounded : 1 O.R. Wounded (Acc.)	
	18th	11.30 p.m.	Battalion relieved by 1/21st Battn LONDON Regt., and marched to billets at WARLOY-BAILLON.	
WARLOY-BAILLON.	19th		Companies at disposal of Coy Commanders for Interior Economy, etc,	
	20th		Interior Economy : Bathing : Pay.	
	21st	10.30 a.m.	Church Parade. Inspection of billets by Commanding Officer.	

2/8/18.   Robert Roberts, Major,
Comdg., 1/23rd Battalion The LONDON Regiment. (T.F.)

Army Form C. 2118.

WAR DIARY
INTELLIGENCE SUMMARY

(Erase heading not required.)

Instructions regarding War Diaries and Intelligence Summaries are contained in F. S. Regs., Part II. and the Staff Manual respectively. Title Pages will be prepared in manuscript.

Place	Date	Hour	Summary of Events and Information	Remarks and references to Appendices
WARLOY.	JULY. 21st	6 p.m.	Battalion relieved 1/24th Battn The LONDON Regt in forward area – COURT SUPPORT & JAKES SUPPORT. H.Qrs at V.22.b.4.7. (Sheet 57 D). 1 O.R. Wounded.	
FORWARD AREA.	24th	11.30 p.m.	H.Qrs., A, B & D Coys relieved 1/20th Battn The LONDON Regt in reserve area of right Brigade. H.Qrs. at V.29.b.9.8.(Sheet 57 D) Coy H.Q. at E.1.a.2.7.(Sheet 62D) C Coy relieved left reserve Coy of 1/18th Battn LONDON Regt.	
	25th		Capt A. Totton, M.C., 18th LONDON Regt appointed Second-in-Command, & assumed duties on 27th July.	
	26th	11.30 p.m.	Battalion relieved 12th Battn The LONDON Regt (175th Bde). H.Qrs at D.12.d.5.8.(Sheet 62D). D Coy ... Right Front Coy. B Coy ... Left Front Coy. A Coy ... Support Coy. C Coy ... Reserve Coy.	
	29th		1 O.R. Wounded.	
	31st	11.30 p.m.	Battalion relieved by 1/24th Battn The LONDON Regt., and marched into Brigade Reserve Area. H.Qrs. at D.5.d.0.3. (Sheet 62 D)	

2nd August, 1918.

Robt A? ?????? Major,
Comdg., 1/23rd Battalion The LONDON Regiment. (T.F.)

142nd Bde.
47th Div.

1/23rd BATTALION,

LONDON REGIMENT,

A U G U S T 1 9 1 8.

Army Form C. 2118.

WAR DIARY
or
INTELLIGENCE SUMMARY
(Erase heading not required.)

1/23rd Bn The London Regt. T.F.

Instructions regarding War Diaries and Intelligence Summaries are contained in F.S. Regs., Part II. and the Staff Manual respectively. Title Pages will be prepared in manuscript.

Place	Date	Hour	Summary of Events and Information	Remarks and references to Appendices
AUGUST, 1918.	1st - 5th.		Battn. in Brigade reserve area near MILLENCOURT - H.Q., D.5.d.0.3.	
	6.		Battn. relieved by 1/21st Bn Lon Regt and moved to trenches between HENENCOURT and SENLIS.	
	7.		Bn. H.Q., and B & D Coys. moved to Billets in WARLOY. A & C Coys. remained under Capt. G.C.PHILLIPS. WARLOY shelled.	
	8.		B & D Coys. refitted, bathed, etc.	
	9.		B & D Coys. relieved A & C Coys. near HENENCOURT; A & C billeted in WARLOY.	
	10.		A & C bathed at WARLOY. Presentation of medal ribbons by Divl. Commander near CONTAY. Sergt. T.H. CARTER received D.C.M. Competition for Brig. General's cup at CONTAY. No 3 Platoon competed.	
	11.		Battn. relieved by 7Th Bn Queen's and moved to LAHOUSSOYE. 2/Lt J.D. FLYNN rejoined from Base.	
	12		Battn. moved to MARETT WOOD, relieving H.Q. Coy. of 130th American Inf. Regt. H.Q. at J.11.a.5.5 (62D). 2/Lts T.E. WOOD & S.R.W. WALKER wounded.	
	13.		Battn. relieved 12th Bn London Regt. H.Q. K.17.a.6.0 (62 D N.E.) near TAILLES WOOD, S.E. of MORLANCOURT. 1 O.R. killed, 3 O.R. wounded. Depot moved to BONNAY. Lt. Col. R.H. TOLERTON, M.C. returned from Fourth Army course and resumed command of Battn. vice Major A. TOTTON, M.C.	
	14.		Battn. relieved by 22nd Bn Lon. Regt. and moved into support in K.10.d. and 16.a. 1 O.R. Killed, 8 O.R. wounded.	
	15.		1 O.R. wounded.	
	16.		2/Lt J.D. FLYNN wounded; 3 O.R. wounded.	

Army Form C. 2118.

WAR DIARY
or
INTELLIGENCE SUMMARY

(Erase heading not required.)

1/23rd Bn The London Regt.

Instructions regarding War Diaries and Intelligence Summaries are contained in F. S. Regs., Part II. and the Staff Manual respectively. Title Pages will be prepared in manuscript.

Place	Date	Hour	Summary of Events and Information	Remarks and references to Appendices
	AUGUST, 1918.			
	17.		Battn. relieved by 17th Bn Lon Regt and moved to area E. of MARETT WOOD. Bn H.Q. at J.11.d.5.3	
	18.		2 O.R. wounded.	
	21.	p.m. 11.40	Battn., relieved by 19th Bn., moved to area E. of HEILLY, with Bn H.Q. at J.13.b.9.3. Battn. bathed in R. ANCRE. Moved to assembly position in area K.10.a.8.2 - K.10.b.3.5 - K.10.d.1.2 - K.10.d.5.4. Bn. H.Q. at K.10.d.3.1.	
	22	3.20 a.m.	Battn. in assembly position. Heavy enemy counter-preparation shell fire during attack by 141st Inf. Bde. ZERO hour 4.45 a.m.	
		5 a.m.	Battn. advanced and passed through line of 141 Inf Bde to line from F.26.b.5.7. - F.27.c.8.7. A, B & D Coys. front line, C Coy. in support 200 yds W. of FORKED TREE (L.2.b.0.9.).	
		8.5 a.m.	Assaulting Coys. advanced to line F.21.c.0.0 - F.21.c.9.0. - F.27.b.15.40 - F.27.b.3.2. - F.27.b.7.0 - F.27.d.2.7., touch being established with 24th Bn on left and 22nd on right. Advd. Bn H.Q. established in HAPPY VALLEY. Casualties moderately heavy.	
		4.35 p.m.	Strong enemy counter-attack turned our left flank; Battn. compelled to withdraw to BROWN LINE - L.1.d.; L.2.c.; L.8.a.	
		10.30 p.m.	142nd Bde relieved by 140 Inf Bde and Battn. withdrew to reserve positions near MARETT WOOD.	
	23.		Refitting. Estimated casualties - 12 Officers, 261 O.R.	
	24.		Coys. moved to area J.12.b. and K.7.a. Battn. H.Q.unchanged. Reorganisation continued.	
	26.		Battn. relieved 21st Bn Lon Regt. in trenches in front of MEAULTE; Battn. H.Q. at F.13.b.5.2. Battle Surplus rejoined from MOILLIENS AU BOIS. Major A. TOTTON, M.C., rejoined and took over duties of Second-in-Command. Capt E.M.PAYNE, M.C., resumed duties of Adjutant vice Lieut G.W. CRISP. Depot moved to MERICOURT L'ABBE.	

Army Form C. 2118.

WAR DIARY
or
INTELLIGENCE SUMMARY

1/23rd Bn The London Regt. T.F.

(Erase heading not required.)

Place	Date	Hour	Summary of Events and Information	Remarks and references to Appendices
	AUGUST, 1918.			
	27		Draft of 300 O.Rs joined Battn. Depot and proceeded to join Battn. in forward area.	
	29		2/Lts R.G. LEE, A.T.URWIN, J.JAFFARY, and L.L.PATERSON joined Battn. in MAMETZ.	
		6 p.m	Battn. moved to neighbourhood of MAMETZ and concentrated in A.7 and F.12, where it rested until nightfall. Battn. moved to area between HARDECOURT-AUX-BOIS and MAUREPAS - B.7.central. H.Q. B.7.d.4.9 Depot moved to MAMETZ.	
	30		142nd Inf. Bde. attacked at 6 a.m. with 23rd Bn. in support. Coys. in B.10.d., B.9.b., Bn H.Q. at B.9.d.2.6. Patrols sent forward to get in touch with front Battalions. 2/Lts C.H.G.ROSS, R.D.SYMONS, A.WHITMARSH, H.R.LEAVER, C.T.THOMAS and A.V. CLEMENTS joined Bn. Casualties 21 O.R., 9 of whom were accidentally wounded by German bomb hidden in the grass. Depot moved to HARDECOURT.	
	31		Battn. remained in Brigade support.	
			NOTE: Officer casualties on 22nd inst:-	
			KILLED. 2/Lt F. CHAPMAN and 2/Lt A.G. SPEARS.	
			WOUNDED. Capt T.E.WEBSTER, H.E.SCOTT, F.H.STARR, R.A. ASKEW, C.B.C.M.LEDGERTON. 2/Lts C.H.G.PHILLIPS, Capt A.J.HARMAN, M.C., 2/Lts. J.H.HORNBY, R.P.GOLDSMITH	
			MISSING. Capt G.C.PHILLIPS, Capt A.J.HARMAN, M.C., 2/Lts. J.H.HORNBY, R.P.GOLDSMITH and H.T. CLEMENTS.	

20.9.18.

J. Cotton
Major,
Commanding, 1/23rd Battn. The London Regiment, T.F.

Army Form C. 2118.

WAR DIARY
or
INTELLIGENCE SUMMARY

(Erase heading not required.)   1/23rd Bn The London Regt. T.F.

Place	Date	Hour	Summary of Events and Information	Remarks and references to Appendices
	SEPTEMBER, 1918.			
	1	a.m. 5.30	47th (London) Division attacked, with 142nd Inf Bde in reserve. "D" Coy. of this Battn. was detailed to mop up PRIEZ FARM. This was successfully carried out. Battn H.Q. moved to B.11.a.4.8. Remainder of the day spent in reorganising. Casualties: 2/Lts R.A.TOMLIN and L.L.PATERSON, Killed; 2/Lt J.H.E.JAFFARY and 12 O.R. wounded.	A.1.
	2	a.m. 5.30	Advance resumed by 142nd Inf. Bde, with Battn. in support. Coys. moved to assembly positions in trenches at C.15.b. and C.9.d. by 4.30 a.m. Rear Battn H.Q. moved to Bde H.Q. at B.11.c.7.1. Adv. Battn H.Q. under Major A.TOTTON, M.C. moved to NEEDLE WOOD, C.13.a.7.2. A Coy. ordered forward to SORROWITZ TRENCH, B Coy. to support of 24th Bn Lon. Regt., and C Coy. to GERMAN WOOD TRENCH. At night Lt A.C.KENNETT rejoined and assumed command of C Coy vice Lt G.W.CRISP. Casualties: Capt C.M.WHEELER wounded. O.R. 7 killed, 28 wounded.	A.1.
	3.		Enemy reported retiring. 2 platoons of C Coy. sent forward as fighting patrol and established posts in CANAL DU NORD, N.E. of MOISLAINS. Advd. Bn H.Q. moved forward to ALF CUT, C.8.d.4.2. C Coy patrol pushed forward and established posts 500 yards E. of CANAL.	A.1.
	4.		Remainder of C Coy., also D Coy., sent forward to reinforce posts already established by C Coy. Enemy concentrating all his artillery on MOISLAINS but no attack developed. Battn H.Q. moved forward to BREMENT TRENCH, C.10.d.9.6.	
	5.		Situation unchanged. Enemy was still holding out in quarries at D.15.a.b. Patrols reported enemy in road running through D.8.b. 141st Inf Bde passed through 142nd Inf Bde. Depot moved to CLERY-SUR-SOMME. A Coy. moved forward to line held by C & D Coys. and established H.Q. with C & D Coys. in CANAL DU NORD.	A.1.
	6.	8 a.m	47th Division attacked, with 142nd Inf Bde in reserve. A, C & D Coys. moved forward to trenches in D.10.a., D.10.c. and D.16.a. and pushed forward patrols to get in touch with 141st Inf Bde. B Coy. moved forward to trenches in D.8.c. Battn H.Q. moved to CANAL DU NORD and at 2 p.m. to VILLE WOOD. Battn. relieved by 8th Bn London Regt, 58th Division, and returned to vicinity of ALF CUT. Since 22/8/18, Battn. had advanced 20 miles.	A.1.

Army Form C. 2118.

WAR DIARY
or
INTELLIGENCE SUMMARY

(Erase heading not required.) 1/23rd Bn The London Regt. T.F.

Instructions regarding War Diaries and Intelligence Summaries are contained in F. S. Regs., Part II. and the Staff Manual respectively. Title Pages will be prepared in manuscript.

Place	Date	Hour	Summary of Events and Information	Remarks and references to Appendices
	SEPTEMBER, 1918.			
	7	p.m.	Battn. moved to CLERY-SUR-SOMME and bathed in R.Somme. Lieut W.IRESON joined from 2/23rd Bn.	
	8	8.30 p.m.	Battn. embussed for MERICOURT, where they bivouacked for the night.	
	9	7.38	Battn. entrained for LILLERS.	
	10	9 a.m	Arrived at LILLERS and marched to ECQUEDECQUES	
	11		Interior economy and general refitting.	
	12	9 a.m	Battn. marched to BURBURE and billeted.	
	13		Route march.RAIMBERT-LOZINGHEM-ALLOUAGNE.	
	14		Battn. fired on 400 yds range near ALLOUAGNE, also bathed at same place.	
	15 to 18		Training in Lewis gun, musketry, steady drill. One Company on range each day. Major A.TOTTON, M.C. took over command from Lt Col R.H.TOLERTON, M.C. (short leave to U.K).	
	19	7.30 a.m.	Battn. marched to BRIAS and billeted.	
	20		Lewis gun and musketry training.	
	21		--do-- 2/Lts R. LIVERMORE, C.H.F.JOHNSON and F.W. RICHARDS joined from Base.	
	22		Sunday. Lieut & Q.M. G.M. WILLIAMS joined from Base.	
	23		2/Lieut R.B.M FIETH joined from Base. Coy. training under own arrangements.	
	24		Parades under Coy. arrangements for musketry, L.G. training and physical drill. Battn. marched to CONTEVILLE in afternoon for Brigade Gymkhana. Notification received of award of 16 Military Medals for recent fighting.	

Army Form C. 2118.

WAR DIARY
or
INTELLIGENCE SUMMARY

(Erase heading not required.) 1/23rd Bn The London Regt. T.F.

Instructions regarding War Diaries and Intelligence Summaries are contained in F.S. Regs., Part II. and the Staff Manual respectively. Title Pages will be prepared in manuscript.

Place	Date	Hour	Summary of Events and Information	Remarks and references to Appendices
	SEPTEMBER, 1918.			
	25		No parades owing to rain. Inspections, lectures, etc. in billets.	
	26		Coy. and Platoon drill, L.G. training, gas drill. C.O. inspected Battalion by Coys. and detachments.	
	27	a.m. 9.30	Battn. paraded and marched to BUNEVILLE and billeted.	
	28		Training under Coy. arrangements. Inspection of rifles by Armourer Staff Sergt.	
	29	a.m. 11	Church parade. Battn. bathed at BUNEVILLE at Baths run under Battn. arrangements.	
	30		Owing to rain, Coys. carried out inspections, etc., in billets.	
	4/10/1918.		J Cotton Major, Commanding, 1/23rd Battn. The London Regiment, T.F.	

Army Form C. 2118.

WAR DIARY
or
INTELLIGENCE SUMMARY

(Erase heading not required.) 1/23rd Battn. The London Regt. T.F.

Instructions regarding War Diaries and Intelligence Summaries are contained in F. S. Regs., Part II. and the Staff Manual respectively. Title Pages will be prepared in manuscript.

Place	Date	Hour	Summary of Events and Information	Remarks and references to Appendices
	OCTOBER, 1918.			
BUNEVILLE	1		Training under Coy. arrangements. Transport moved to NADONCHELLE for night, to proceed to LESTREM area on 2nd inst.	
	2		Battn. entrained at ST POL for MERVILLE, marched to LA GORGUE and bivouacked for night.	
	3		Battn. moved to LE TILLELOY. Brigade in support to advance of 141st Inf. Bde. Battn. moved to 1st objective, N. of LES CLOCHERS.	
	4	12.45	Battn. moved to LE MAISNIL. Brigade passed through the right of 141st Inf. Bde. 22nd Bn. front, 24th Bn support, 23rd Bn. reserve. Brigade 'phoned, ordering two Companies to form defensive flank on right of 22nd Bn. "B" and "D" Coys. detailed. Battn. ordered to push forward patrols E. of BEAUCAMPS. A & C Coys. at LE MAISNIL. 1 O.R. killed, 4 O.R. wounded.	
	5		Brigade front reorganised. "C" Coy. moved up to ORKNEY TRENCH in support. 1 O.R. killed. Lt Col. R.H.TOLERTON, M.C. rejoined from leave.	
	6		"A" Coy. moved to O.20.d. in reserve. Daylight patrols sent to RAILWAY EMBANKMENT to ascertain whether enemy retirement had commenced. Enemy still held previous positions. 5 O.R. killed, 10 O.R. wounded. "C" relieved "D", "A" Coy relieved "B".	
	7		In line E. of BEAUCAMPS.	
	8	Night.	Divl. front reorganised. "A" Coy's position taken over by 24th Bn R.W.F. (74th Division). 1 O.R. killed.	
		Night.	Battn. relieved by 22nd Bn. "C" Coy. relieved by platoon of 22nd Bn. During relief enemy tried to raid one of our posts but was driven off. Relief proceeded without any further trouble. "C" Coy. moved back to area, near LE MAISNIL with "B" Coy. "A" and "D" occupied 2nd line system. Battn H.Q. moved to LE MAISNIL. 2 O.R. wounded.	
	9.		Battn. in support.	
	10.		Battn. in support.	

Army Form C. 2118.

WAR DIARY
or
INTELLIGENCE SUMMARY

(Erase heading not required.)   1/23rd Bn. The London Regt. T.F.

Instructions regarding War Diaries and Intelligence Summaries are contained in F.S. Regs., Part II. and the Staff Manual respectively. Title Pages will be prepared in manuscript.

Place	Date	Hour	Summary of Events and Information	Remarks and references to Appendices
	OCTOBER, 1918.			
	11.		"B" relieved "A" in 2nd line, and "C" relieved "D". 1 O.R. wounded.	
	12.		"C" moved back to positions near LE MAISNIL.	
	13.		"A" and "D" Coys. bathed at farm, O.20.a.5.7. 2/Lt. E.M.HORNER sick to Hospl.	
	14.	Night.	"C", "B" and H.Q. bathed. Coy. Comdrs. reconnoitred line of 22nd Bn. Battn. relieved 22nd Bn in front line. D Coy left, A Coy right, front line; B Coy support, "C" reserve. Advd. Bn. H.Q., Chateau de Flandre.	
		2350	Wire from Division: "German wireless message intercepted tonight gives orders to troops on "this front to withdraw tonight". Message repeated to Coys. and special vigilance ordered.	
	15	0258	Wire from A Coy. states enemy still in position. patrols still out.	
		0655	A Coy. platoon patrol out to reach Railway Embankment.	
		0810	Brigade Major 'phones to say 74th Division have reached Railway Embankment. Forward Coys. notified.	
		0820	A Coy. moved forward to Railway Embankment as per scheme "A" and pushed forward patrols. D Coy. moved forward to conform.	
		0905	Scheme "A" put into effect.	
		1005	"A" Coy. held up by M.G. at O.17.c.9.8. Coy. H.Q. moved to O.16.d.0.1. Left of 74th Div. O.17.d.9.8.	
		1010	Bde informed of above.	
		1040	Rear Bn H.Q. moved to Chateau. "B" front line, "C" Coy at Chateau.	
		1130	Verbal report given to Brigadier by C.O. " D Coy. patrols report FIN de la GUERRE cleared of enemy. A Coy. patrol held up by M.G. at strong point O.17.d.; patrols pushing round. Main line E. of railway".	
		1220	Amendment to Appendix A received.	
		1225	Advd. Bn H.Q. established at O.17.c.25.70.	
		1255	First objective gained.	
		1300	Liaison Officer reported situation on right - 14th Royal Highlanders (74th Div.).	
		1315	Amendment to Appendix A recd. and substance communicated to Advd. Bn H.Q.	
		1315	Right Coy. reported they were held up by M.G. and snipers from O.24.b.8.3. Artillery support called for.	

Army Form C. 2118.

WAR DIARY
or
INTELLIGENCE SUMMARY

(Erase heading not required.) 1/23rd Bn The London Regt. T.F.

Instructions regarding War Diaries and Intelligence Summaries are contained in F. S. Regs., Part II. and the Staff Manual respectively. Title Pages will be prepared in manuscript.

Place	Date	Hour	Summary of Events and Information	Remarks and references to Appendices
	OCTOBER, 1918.			
	15	1340	C.O. reported to Brigade by 'phone that front Coys. were moving up to 2nd objective. "B" Coy.	
		1550	Bde. ordered patrol to be sent to ESCOOBECQUES to ascertain whether clear of enemy. "B" Coy. detailed.	
		1430	B Coy. ordered to move to Railway Embankment and "C" Coy. to old British outpost line.	
		1440	D Coy. (left Coy) reported to be held up by M.G. and snipers from right	
			Rear Battn H.Q. moved to 0.17.c.25.70.	
		1520	Report recd. from A Coy. giving dispositions. Still held up but gradually pushing round flanks.	
		1530	Artillery informed verbally and support called for on M.G. posts, etc.	
		1545	A Coy. informed of proposed action of Arty.	
		1650	Patrols reported ESCOBECQUE clear of enemy; Brigade informed by wire.	
		1700	Artillery opened on M.G. posts. One battery detailed by Bde opened on trenches O.12.central to O.18. central. Front Coys. advanced under cover of shelling.	
		1725	Objective reached. Enemy left trenches and ran back.	
		1930	One platoon of "B" Coy. ordered up to support A Coy. - in position 2120.	
		2015	Divl. Commander's congratulations received over phone and sent to Coys.	
		2200	Orders from Bde. stating that advance would continue on the morrow. 22nd and 24th Bns. to pass through 23rd Bn, who would remain in present position and become Bde. reserve.	
			3 O.R. killed, 8 O.R. wounded.	
	16	1145	B & C Coys. ordered up to positions W. of Fort d'ENGIOS to support 22nd Bn. Support and Reserve Coys. of 22nd Bn moving to high ground P.l.	
		1500	Move completed.	
	17.		Battn. moved to FROMELLES. Dinner at Fromelles and entrained for BOUT DEVILLE.	
	18.		Battn. moved by march route to LA PIERRIERE and billeted.	
	19.		Interior Economy.	
	20.		Church Parade. Notification received of award of 5 M.C's and 15 M.M.'s	
	21.		Battn. moved to BUSNES and billeted.	

Army Form C. 2118.

WAR DIARY
or
INTELLIGENCE SUMMARY

(Erase heading not required.)

1/23rd Bn The London Regt. T.F.

Instructions regarding War Diaries and Intelligence Summaries are contained in F.S. Regs., Part II. and the Staff Manual respectively. Title Pages will be prepared in manuscript.

Place	Date	Hour	Summary of Events and Information	Remarks and references to Appendices
	OCTOBER, 1918.			
BUSNES	22	0830	Training under Coy. arrangements. Draft of 10 O.R. from Base.	
	23	0830 – 1230	Training under Coy. arrangements. 2/Lt E.E.CHOSLEY rejoined from III Corps School. Bn. marched to ST VENANT area and carried out tactical scheme.	
	24	0830 – 1245	Training under Coy. arrangements. Baths in Chateau grounds. 6 O.R. from Base.	
	25	0830 1115	Coy. inspections, etc. Battn. paraded in Chateau grounds for presentation of medal ribbons by Div. Commander. Baths in Chateau grounds. Notification received of award of 1 M.C., 1 D.C.M. and 1 bar to M.M.	
	26	1015	Battn. paraded and marched ILLIERS, entrained to DON and marched to billets in LOOS, near LILLE, the Battn. being the first British troops to be billeted there since its liberation. Whole of Battn. and Transport billeted in a factory.	
	27		Interior economy, cleaning up, etc.	
	28	0900	Battn. paraded and marched to rendezvous of 142nd Inf Bde outside LILLE. 47th (London) Division marched through LILLE on the occasion of the oficial entry into the City of G.O.C. Commanding Fifth Army. 142 Inf Bde headed the procession; 23rd Bn. was second Infantry Battn. to enter the City. Enthusiastic welcome received. Battn. afterwards marched to LEZENNES and billeted.	
	29	0900	Battn. and Company training.	
	30	1100	Brigade inspected by B.G.C.	
	31	0900 – 12.30.	Battn. and Coy. training, including ceremonial and march past.	

2/11/18.

Lt. Colonel,
Comdg., 1/23rd Bn. The London Regiment.

Army Form C. 2118.

WAR DIARY
or
INTELLIGENCE SUMMARY

(Erase heading not required.) 1/23rd Bn The London Regt. T.F.

Instructions regarding War Diaries and Intelligence Summaries are contained in F.S. Regs., Part II. and the Staff Manual respectively. Title Pages will be prepared in manuscript.

142/47

Place	Date	Hour	Summary of Events and Information	Remarks and references to Appendices
	NOVEMBER, 1918.			
WILLEMS	1	0815	Battn. paraded and marched to WILLEMS, and billeted.	
	2	0900	Coy. etc training under own arrangements.	
	3	0945	Divine Service. Inspection of billets by Commanding Officer.	
	4	0900	Coy. etc training. Lewis gun, Scout, and specialist training.	
	5	0900	Coy. and Specialist Training.	
		1430	Battn. Boxing Competition. Draft of 21 O.R. from Base.	
	6		Battn. prepared to move up into Support area, but move was postponed until next day.	
	7		2 Platoons of 35th Bn, Portuguese Infantry, attached to Battn. for instruction. 1 platoon with B and D Coys.	
		1600	Battn. moved up to Support, relieving 20th Bn London Regt., on TOURNAI front.	
	8		Battn. crossed R. ESCAUT. Billets for night at MOORCOURT	
	9			
	10		Battn. marched to FRASNES. and formed outpost line to East of the town. Transport joined Bn during the evening.	
FRASNES	11	0930	Battn. paraded to march to KAIN.	
		1100	News received that the German delegates had signed the Armistice terms. No demonstration ensued.	
		1630	Battn. arrived at KAIN and billeted.	
	12		Interior Economy.	
	13		Inspections and physical training. Notification received of award of 12 M.Ms for work in connection with Operations in front of LILLE.	

Army Form C. 2118.

WAR DIARY
or
INTELLIGENCE SUMMARY

(Erase heading not required.)   1/23rd Bn The London Regt T.F.

Instructions regarding War Diaries and Intelligence Summaries are contained in F. S. Regs., Part II. and the Staff Manual respectively. Title Pages will be prepared in manuscript.

Place	Date	Hour	Summary of Events and Information	Remarks and references to Appendices
	NOVEMBER, 1918.			
KAIN	14	0900	Inspections, physical drill, Coy and Platoon drill.	
		1000	Portuguese troops attached paraded and marched off to rejoin their Battn at BIZENCOURT. Band played them to destination.	
		1030	Coys. carried out short route march.	
	15	1000	Battn. paraded and marched to CYSOING.	
CYSOING.	16		Interior Economy.	
	17	0900	Divine Service in Cinema. General Purposes Committee formed to control Sports, recreations, Canteen, etc.	
	18	0900	Inspection, physical drill, Coy. drill and short route marches, all under Company and Detachment Commanders. 2/Lt H.A.V. MORETON, M.C., rejoined Battn from Base. Posted to "B" Coy.	
	19	0900	Parades as yesterday.	
	20	0900	--do-- Armr. Sergt. inspected the Lewis guns of Battn.	
		1030	Junior N.C.Os' class under R.S.M. in guard duties.	
	21	0900	Parades as yesterday.	
		1030	Junior N.C.Os' class under R.S.M. Educational Classes formed with hin the Battn. 2/Lt C.T. THOMAS apptd Educational Officer.	
	22	0900	Coy. Inspections, physical drill, close order drill, Lewis gun training, scouting, &c.	
	23	0900	Parades as yesterday. T/Lieut A.A. le Poer-Power awarded M.C. 23rd Battn, 3rd. Brigade Cross-country run.	
	24	1100	Divine Service. Transport of Brigade inspected by B.G.C. 23rd Bn won the Competition.	

2449 Wt. W14957/Mgo 750,000 1/16 J.B.C. & A. Forms/C.2118/12.

Army Form C. 2118.

WAR DIARY
or
INTELLIGENCE SUMMARY

(Erase heading not required.) 1/23rd Bn The London Regt. T.F.

Instructions regarding War Diaries and Intelligence Summaries are contained in F.S. Regs., Part II. and the Staff Manual respectively. Title Pages will be prepared in manuscript.

Place	Date	Hour	Summary of Events and Information	Remarks and references to Appendices
	NOVEMBER, 1918.			
	25	0930	Battn. paraded and marched to HAUBOURDIN area and billeted for night. Lieuts E.R.GURTON and R.J.MACKAY joined from Base.	
	26	0830	Battn. paraded and marched to BETHUNE (Tobacco Factory) and billeted for night.	
	27	0900	Battn. paraded and marched to BURBURE and billeted.	
BURBURE	28		Coys. paraded under own arrangements.	
	29		--do--	
	30	0900	Coy. inspection; physical drill, close order drill Educational classes resumed.	
	3/12/18.			

Lieut. Colonel,

Comdg., 1/23rd Battn. The London Regiment, T.F.

Army Form C. 2118.

WAR DIARY
or
INTELLIGENCE SUMMARY
(Erase heading not required.)

1/23rd Battn. The London Regt.

Instructions regarding War Diaries and Intelligence Summaries are contained in F. S. Regs, Part II. and the Staff Manual respectively. Title Pages will be prepared in manuscript.

Vol 46

Place	Date	Hour	Summary of Events and Information	Remarks and references to Appendices
BURBURE.	DECEMBER, 1918.			
	1	1045	Divine Service in Y.M.C.A. Hut, Lillers.	
	2	0900	Coy. drill, inspections, etc.	
	3	0900	Physical drill, etc. 1015. Route march.	
	4	0900	Coy. inspections, etc. 1030. Route march.	
	5	0900	Coy. parades for physical drill, etc. Battn. found BUTT party for Brigade Rifle Meeting. 1Lieut. W.A. Solven and 2/Lt A.F. Huggons joined from Base. No 13 platoon won "Daily Telegraph" Cup & medals in Brigade Competition.	
	6	0900	Coy. drill, physical drill, etc.	
	7	0900 0830	Inspections, physical drill - 1230. Battn. bathed at Allouagne. 3 men despatched to Transportation Troops, Calais.	
	8	1000	Divine service. 1Lieut A.J. PIGGOTT joined from Base.	
	9	0900 1030	Physical drill, sentry drill, inspections, etc. under Coy. arrangements. Separate office formed to deal with Demobilisation, under Capt S.A. GRAY, M.C. Route march. 6 O.R. from Base.	
	10	0900	Coy. parades. 1030. Route march. (Party consisting of 2/Lts I.J. Phillips & R.B. Fleth, 5 men to Dispersal centre. (R.S.M. G.J.Small, and Sergts DEVITT and PAINE proceeded (to U.K. for the Colours.	
	11	0900	Coy. parades. 1030. Route march.	
	12	0900	Coy. Parades. During morning details for Demobilisation taken for each man.	
	13	0900	Coy. inspections, etc. 1030. Route march.	

Army Form C. 2118.

WAR DIARY
or
INTELLIGENCE SUMMARY

(Erase heading not required.) 1/23rd Bn The London Regt.

Instructions regarding War Diaries and Intelligence Summaries are contained in F. S. Regs., Part II. and the Staff Manual respectively. Title Pages will be prepared in manuscript.

Place	Date	Hour	Summary of Events and Information	Remarks and references to Appendices
BURBURE.	DECEMBER 1918.			
	14	0900	Coy. inspections, etc. Battn. bathed at Illers. 13 men to Dispersal centre.	
	15	1000	Divine Service. Lieut. A.W. DURRANT, D.S.O., from Base. 39 men to Dispersal centre.	
	16	0900	Physical drill, Coy. drill, etc. 1030. Route march. Capt G.W. Crisp, M.C. and 2/Lts P.W. WRIGHT and F.W. RICHARDS sick to Hpl.	
	17	0930	Practise Inspection on Recreation ground. 1030. Route march. Capt W. IRESON sick to Hpl. Major A. Totton, M.C., to Hpl.	
	18	0830	Battn. paraded and marched to Aerodrome at Auchel for inspection by Brigadier. Colour party returned from England with Colours.	
	19	0900	Battn. paraded and marched to Aerodrome at Auchel to rehearse march past, etc.	
	20	0830	Battn. marched to Auchel for inspection by Brigadier.	
	21	0900	Physical drill, Coy. drill, etc. 1030. Route march.	
	22	1000	Divine Service. 7 men to Dispersal Centre.	
	23	0900	Physical drill, close order drill, etc. Bathing under Coy. arrangements at BURBURE. 5 men to Dispersal centre.	
	24	0900	Coy. parades. General interior economy.	
	25		Christmas Day. Coys. made own arrangements for dinners, concerts, etc. 11 men to Dispersal Centre.	
	26		Clearing up billets. Battn. Concert Party (formed by Lieut. R.J. MACKAY) gave their first performance.	Sgt. C.T. HARRINGTON M.M.

Army Form C. 2118.

WAR DIARY
or
INTELLIGENCE SUMMARY

(Erase heading not required.) 1/23rd Bn. The London Regt.

Instructions regarding War Diaries and Intelligence Summaries are contained in F.S. Regs., Part II. and the Staff Manual respectively. Title Pages will be prepared in manuscript.

Place	Date	Hour	Summary of Events and Information	Remarks and references to Appendices
	DECEMBER, 1918.			
BURBURE.	26 27	0900. 0930	Coys. paraded for inspection. Battn. paraded for route march.	
	28	0900	Interior economy, changing over billets (B Coy), drainage of Camp (D Coy). etc. 1 man to Dispersal Centre.	
	29	1100	Divine service.	
	30	0930	Battn. paraded for route march.	
	31	0900 0930	Coy. inspections, etc. Route march.	
			During the month of DECEMBER, Educational classes were held daily from 1030 to 1200.	
			During the greater part of the month, Battn. supplied working parties erecting a Hutted Camp on Burbure-Allouagne road.	

3rd January 1919.

[signature]
Lieut. Colonel,
Comdg., 1/23rd Battn. The London Regiment, T.F.

Army Form C. 2118.

WAR DIARY
or
INTELLIGENCE SUMMARY

(Erase heading not required.) 1/23rd Battn The London Regt.

Instructions regarding War Diaries and Intelligence Summaries are contained in F. S. Regs., Part II. and the Staff Manual respectively. Title Pages will be prepared in manuscript.

Place	Date	Hour	Summary of Events and Information	Remarks and references to Appendices
JANUARY 1919.				
BURBURE.	1	0900	Coy. inspections 0930 Route march .	
	2	0900	Coy. inspections . 0930 Route march . Capt. G.W. Crisp, M.C. returned from hospital. Bn Boxing Class commenced under directions of C.S.M. King, M.M.	
	3	0900	Coy. inspections : 0930 Route march . 2/Lieut. A.V. Clements Conducting Officer . 4 O.R. to Dispersal Centre :	
	4	0900	Coy. inspections . 0930 Route march .	
	5	1045	Divine Service in Y.M.C.A. Hut, Tillers . Major A. Totton, M.C. returned from hospital . Sergt. Jackson cross-posted from 1/17th Battn. .	
	6	0900	Coy. inspections .0930 Route march . Pay . 2/Lieut F.W. Richards transferred to U.K. (Sick).	
	7	0900	Coy. inspections . 0930 Route march . 2/Lieut. D.T. Newton returned from leave .	
	8	0900	Coy. inspections . Work on PIACE, roads and entrance to Bn Recreation Ground .	
	9	0915	Brigade Route march . Capt. A.W. Durrant, D.S.O. returned from leave .	
	10	0900	Coy. inspections . 0930 Route march . Lieut. H.H. Henthorne returned from leave . 5 O.R. to Dispersal Centre .	
	11	0900	Coy. inspections . 0930 Route march . 7 O.R. to Dispersal Centre.	
	12	0930	Divine Service in Y.M.C.A. Hut, Tillers . Lieut P.H. Hughes appointed B.T.O. 2/Lieut. W.G. Irwin Conducting Officer. 9 P.R. to Dispersal Centre. and struck off strength.	

Army Form C. 2118.

WAR DIARY
or
INTELLIGENCE SUMMARY

(Erase heading not required.)   1/23rd Bn The London Regt.

Instructions regarding War Diaries and Intelligence Summaries are contained in F.S. Regs., Part II. and the Staff Manual respectively. Title Pages will be prepared in manuscript.

Place	Date	Hour	Summary of Events and Information	Remarks and references to Appendices
JANUARY 1919.				
BURBURE.	13	0900	Coy. inspections. 0945 Route march. Pay. 2/Lieut. R.H. Brewster Conducting officer. 15 O.R. to Dispersal Centre.	
	14	0900	Coy. inspections. Salvage work. 2/Lieut I.M. Whyte left Unit for demobilization. Guard Room established in Camp. 14 O.R. to Dispersal Centre.	
	15	0900	Coy. inspections. 1040 Brigade Route march. 1 O.R. from Base.	
	16	0900	Coy. inspections. Salvage work. 3 men from each Coy. transferred to Transport Section.	
	17	0900	Coy. inspections. Salvage work. Capt. E.M. Payne, M.C., Capt. S.A. Gray, M.C. and 2/Lieut. J.I. Swabey left Unit for demobilization. 2/Lieut. C.R.F. Johnson and 2/Lieut R. Livermore Conducting officers. 19 O.R. to Dispersal Centre.	
	18	0900	Coy. inspections. interior economy, bathing and kit inspections under Coy. arrangements. B.Coy. moved into Camp. Lieut.-Col R.H. Tolerton, M.C. proceeded on short leave to U.K. and Major A. Totten, M.C. assumed Command of Battalion. Capt. M.W. Robertson, (M.C.,R.C.)U.S.A. left Battn. to rejoin A.E.F. 12 O.R. to Dispersal Centre. 10.R. from Base.	
	19	0950	Divine Service in Y.M.C.A. Hut, Lillers. 2/Lieut. E.B. Fleth Conducting Officer. 23 O.R. to Dispersal Centre.	
	20	0900	Coy. inspections. 0930 Route march Capt. W Ireson Conducting officer. 12 O.R. to Dispersal Camp. Pay.	
	21	0900	Coy. inspections. All available men employed on work in Camp. 2/Lieut. I.J. Phillips Conducting Officer. 13 O.R. to Dispersal Centre.	
	22	0900	Brigade Parade. Major E.W. Mayhew, M.C. attached for duty as 2nd-in-Command.	

Army Form C. 2118.

WAR DIARY
or
INTELLIGENCE SUMMARY
(Erase heading not required.) 1/23rd Battn The London Regt.

Instructions regarding War Diaries and Intelligence Summaries are contained in F. S. Regs., Part II. and the Staff Manual respectively. Title Pages will be prepared in manuscript.

Place	Date	Hour	Summary of Events and Information	Remarks and references to Appendices
JANUARY 1919				
BURBURE.	23	0900	Coy. inspections. All available men at work on Camp. C.Coy. moved into Camp.	
	24	0900	Coy. inspections. " " " " " " 20 P.R. to Dispersal Centre.	
	25	0900	Interior economy, bathing and kit inspections under Coy. arrangements. 24 O.R. to Dispersal Centre.	
	26	1015	Divine Service in BattN, Recreation Room. 23 O.R. to Dispersal Centre.	
	27	0900	Company inspections. All available men at work on Camp. A.Coy. moved into camp. 20 O.R. to Dispersal Centre.	
	28	0900	Company inspections. All available men at work on Camp. 2/Lieut. H.A.V. Moreton, M.C. Conducting Officer. 19 O.R. to Dispersal Centre.	
	29	0900	Coy. inspections. All available men at work on Camp.	
	30	0900	Coy. inspections. " " " " " "	
	31	0900	Coy. inspections. " " " " " " Lieut. E.E. Choseley Conducting Officer. 13 O.R. to Dispersal Camp.	

During the month of January, Educational classes were held daily with the exception of Wednesdays.
During the month of January 53 O.R. were demobilized whilst on leave in U.K.

4th. February 1919.

Bolton
Major,
Com'dg. 1/23rd Battn. The London Regiment T.F.

Army Form C. 2118.

WAR DIARY
or
INTELLIGENCE SUMMARY

(Erase heading not required.)

1/23rd. Battn. The London Regiment.

Vol 48

Place	Date	Hour	Summary of Events and Information	Remarks and references to Appendices
FEBRUARY 1919. BURBURE.	1	0900	Company Inspections. 1030 Educational Classes. Kit Inspections, Lewis Gun Inspection and Bathing etc. Work on Officers' Camp. "D" Company moved to ST. PIERRIETTE for duty as Guard. Orderly 4oom and Aid Post established in Camp. H.Q. Company moved into Camp. 22 Other Ranks left unit for Dispersal Centre.	
	2	1030	Divine Service in Dining Hall. Lieut. R.J. MACKAY proceeded to ROUBAIX to attend Course. 19 Other Ranks left Unit for Dispersal Centre. 2 O.R. proceeded to ETAPLES for duty as Clerks.	
	3	0900	Company Inspections. Work on Camps etc. Pay. Lieut. H.H. HENTHORNE proceeded to 236th. Bde, R.F.A. for duty as Instructor.	
	4	0900	Company Inspections. Work on Camps etc. Q.M. Stores established in Camp. Lieut. W.A. SOLVEN proceeded to U.K. on leave.	
	5	0900	Company Inspections. Work on Camps etc. Lieut. E.R. GURTON left unit for Draft Conducting Duties and leave. 20 Other Ranks left unit for Dispersal Centre.	
	6	0900	Company Inspections. Work on Camps etc. 21 Other Ranks left unit for Dispersal Centre.	
	7	0900	Company Inspections. Work on Camps. Capt. A.C. KENNETT, Lieut. H.W. FIETH, Lieut. A.F. HUGGONS, 2/Lieut. L.F. FISHER, 2/Lieut. D.T. NEWTON, 2/Lieut. C.H.G. ROSS and 114 Other Ranks transferred to 2/23rd. Bn The lond on Regt. Educational Classes ceased. 14 Other Ranks left unit for Dispersal Centre.	
	8	0900	Company Inspections. Work on Camps. Kit Inspections, Bathing etc. 9 Other Ranks left unit for Dispersal Centre.	

2449 Wt. W14957/M90 750,000 1/16 J.B.C. & A. Forms/C.2118/12.

Army Form C. 2118.

WAR DIARY
or
INTELLIGENCE SUMMARY

(Erase heading not required.) 1/23rd. Battn. The London Regiment.

Instructions regarding War Diaries and Intelligence Summaries are contained in F.S. Regs., Part II. and the Staff Manual respectively. Title Pages will be prepared in manuscript.

Place	Date	Hour	Summary of Events and Information	Remarks and references to Appendices
FEBRUARY 1919.				
BURBURE.	9	0930	Divine Service in Battn. Recreation Room. 4 Other Ranks left unit for Dispersal Centre.	
	10	0900	Company Inspections. Work on Camps. 2/Lieut. A.V. CLEMENTS returned from leave. Pay.	
	11	0900	Company Inspections. Work on Camps. 2/Lieut. R.H. BREWSTER returned from leave.	
	12	0900	Company Inspections. Work on Camps. Lieut. Col. R.H. TOKERTON, M.C. returned from leave and assumed Command of Battalion. 42286 (now 705307) Pte G. McManam sentenced to 120 days I.H.L. 1 Other Rank left unit for Dispersal Centre.	
	13	0900	Company Inspections. 2/Lieut. R. LIVERMORE returned from leave. 3 Other Ranks left unit for Dispersal Centre. 2/Lieut. R.B. FLETH returned from leave. Officers' Mess established in Camp. Work on Camps.	
	14	0900	Company Inspections. All Officers moved into Camp. Work on Camps. 2/Lieuts. W.G. IRWIN and T.J. PHILLIPS returned from leave. Padre left unit for duty with 236th. Bde, R.F.A. Lieut. P.C. HUGHES relinquishes appointment of B.T.O. and taken on strength of Battalion. 6 Other Ranks left unit for Dispersal Centre.	
	15	0900	Company Inspections. Work on Camp. Kit Inspections, Bathing etc. 2 Other Ranks left unit for Dispersal Centre.	
	16	1000	Divine Service with R.E's at RAIMBERT.	
	17	0900	Company Inspections. Work on Camps. Pay.	
	18	0900	Company Inspections. Work on Camps.	
	19	0900	Company Inspections. Work on Camps. 4 Other Ranks left unit for Dispersal Centre.	

Army Form C. 2118.

WAR DIARY
or
INTELLIGENCE SUMMARY

(Erase heading not required.) 1/23rd. Battn The London Regiment.

Instructions regarding War Diaries and Intelligence Summaries are contained in F. S. Regs., Part II. and the Staff Manual respectively. Title Pages will be prepared in manuscript.

Place	Date	Hour	Summary of Events and Information	Remarks and references to Appendices
FEBRUARY 1919.				
BURBURE.	20	0900	Company Inspections. Work on Camps. Major A. TOTTON, M.C. left unit for Draft Conducting Duties and Leave. 2/Lieut. C.H.F. JOHNSON returned from leave. 4 O.R. left Unit for Dispersal Centre. G42286 (now 705307) Pte G.McManam's Sentence (120days I.H.L)Commuted to 90 days F.P. NO; 2.	
	21	0900	Company Inspections. Work on Camps. 6 Other Ranks left unit for Dispersal Centre.	
	22	0900	Company Inspections. Work on Camps. Kit Inspections, Bathing etc. Major E.W. MAYHEW, M.C. (22nd. Battn.) attd. Sick to Hospital. 2/Lieut. E.E. GHOSLEY returned from leave. 4 O.R. left unit foe D.C.	
	23	1130	Divine Service in Battn. Recreation Room. Capt. W IRESON and Lieut. W.A. SOLVEN returned from leave. R.S.M. G.J. SMALL and 2 O.R. left UNIT for Dispersal Centre.	
	24	0900	Inspections. Coy. Drill. Work on Camp. Pay.	
	25	0900	Inspections. Physical Training. 2/Lieut. H.A.V. MORETON, M.C. returned from leave. Work on Camp.	
	26	0900	Inspections. 2 hours on Range, ALLOUAGNE. 4 O.R. left unit for Dispersal Centre.	
	27.	0900	Inspections. Physical Training. Work on Camp. 2 O.R. left Unit for Dispersal Centre.	
	28	0900	Inspections. Physical Training. Work on Camp. 2/Lieut. E.R. GURTON returned from leave.	

Lieut. Col.,

Comdg. 1/23rd. Battn. The London Regiment.

Army Form C. 2118.

WAR DIARY
or
INTELLIGENCE SUMMARY.
(Erase heading not required.)

1/23rd Battn The London Regiment.

Place	Date	Hour	Summary of Events and Information	Remarks and references to Appendices
BURBURE. March	1	0900	Inspection, Baths, Kit Inspections and Interior Economy.	
	2	1100	Divine Service - R.E. Camp, Burbure. Lieut. R.J. Mackay posted to 1/9th. Bn London Regt. Lieut. E.R. Garton posted to 1/12th Bn London Rgt. Lt. A.T. Piggott Draft Duties and leave.	
	3	0900	Inspection and Physical Training. Pay. 2/ Lt.G. Huxtable returned from Divl. Rest Camp.	
		1030	Court of Enquiry held in Camp.	
	4	0900	Inspection and Physical Training.	
	5	0900	Inspection and Physical Training.	
	6	0900	Inspection and Drill.	
	7	0900	Inspection and Physical Training.	
	8	0900	Inspection, Baths, Kit Inspections and Interior Economy.	
	9	1030	Divine Service - R.E. Camp, Burbure.	
	10	0900	Inspection and Drill. Pay.	
	11	0900	Inspection and Physical Training.	
	12	0900	Inspection and Physical Training.	
	13	0900	Inspection and Physical Training.	
	14	0900	Inspection and Physical Training.	
	15	0900	Inspection, Baths, Kit Inspections, and Interior Economy. Court of Enquiry re-assembled.	
	16	1030	Divine Service - R.E. Camp, Burbure. 1 O.R. left unit for Dispersal Centre.	

Army Form C. 2118.

WAR DIARY
or
INTELLIGENCE SUMMARY.

(Erase heading not required.) 1/23rd Battn The London Regiment.

Instructions regarding War Diaries and Intelligence Summaries are contained in F. S. Regs., Part II. and the Staff Manual respectively. Title pages will be prepared in manuscript.

Place	Date	Hour	Summary of Events and Information	Remarks and references to Appendices
BURBURE. March.	17	0900	Inspection and Physical Training. Pay.	
	18	0900	Inspection and Physical Training.	
	19	0900	Inspection and Physical Training. 1 O.R. left unit for Dispersal Centre.	
	20	0900	Inspection and Physical Training.	
	21	0900	Inspection and Physical Training.	
	22	0900	Inspection, Baths, Kit Inspections and Interior Economy.	
	23	1130	Divine Service - R.E. Camp, Burbure.	
	24	0900	Inspection and Physical Training. Pay. Lt. A.J. Piggott returned from leave.	
	25	0900	Inspection and Physical Training. Capt. W. Ireson left unit for Demobilization.	
	26	0900	Inspection and Physical Training. 3 O.R. left unit for Dispersal Centre.	
	27	0900	Inspection. 0915 Route March.	
	28	0900	Inspection. 1000 Battn. paraded and marched to FLORINGHEM Aerodrome for farewell address by Div'l. Commdr.	
	29	0900	Inspection, Kit Inspections and Interior Economy	
	30	1000	Divine Service - R.E. Camp, Burbure.	
	31	0900	Inspection and Physical Training. Pay. Capt. Crisp, M.O., Lt. A.J. Piggott & 2/Lt. R.H. Brewster left unit for Demobilization.	

Comdg. 1/23rd Bn The London Regt,
Lieut. Colonel,

Army Form C. 2118.

WAR DIARY
or
INTELLIGENCE SUMMARY

(Erase heading not required.)

1/23rd. Battn. The London Regiment. T.F.

Instructions regarding War Diaries and Intelligence Summaries are contained in F. S. Regs., Part II. and the Staff Manual respectively. Title Pages will be prepared in manuscript.

Place	Date	Hour	Summary of Events and Information	Remarks and references to Appendices
BURBURE	April 1		Inspection and Physical Training.	
	2		Inspection. Route March.	
	3		Inspection and Physical Training.	
	4		Inspection and Route March. Court of Enquiry held in Camp.	
	5		Interior Economy, Baths and Kit Inspections. 2/Lts.- G. Huxtable & A.V. Clements left unit for Demobilization. 2 O.R's left unit for Dispersal Centre.	
	6		Divine Service. Major E.W. Mayhew, M.C.(22nd. Bn.) returned from Sick Leave.	
	7		Inspection and Physical Training. Pay.	
	8		Inspection and Route March.	
	9		Inspection and Physical Training.	
	10		Inspection and Physical Training.	
	11		Inspection and Physical Training. Major A. Totton, M.C. & Major E.W. Mayhew, M.C. left unit for Demobilization.	
	12		Inspection. Baths, Interior Economy and Kit Inspections.	
	13		Church Services. 1 O.R. left unit for Dispersal Centre.	
	14		Inspection and Physical Training. Pay. Lieut. W.G. Irwin & 2/Lts E.E. Chosley & R. Tivermore left unit for Demobilization.	
	15		Inspection and Physical Training. 2/Lts I.J. Phillips, H.A.V. Moreton, M.C. & O.H.E. Johnson, and 40 O.R's transferred to the 2/23rd. Bn. The London Regiment. 17 O.R's left unit for Dispersal Centre.	
	16		Inspection and Work on Camp. Lieut. W.A. Solven left unit for 47th. Divl. Coy.	
	17		Battn. moved to FLORINGHEM Camp.	
FLORINGHEM	18		Fatigues etc.	
	19		Guards. All available O.R's bathed at PERNES	
	20		Fatigues.	
	21		"	
	22		Guards etc.	
	23		Fatigues. Pay.	
	24		"	
	25		Guards.	
	26		Fatigues.	
	27		"	
	28		Cadre entrained at Pernes.	

Army Form C. 2118.

WAR DIARY
or
INTELLIGENCE SUMMARY

(Erase heading not required.)

1/23rd. Battn. The London Regt.

Place	Date	Hour	Summary of Events and Information	Remarks and references to Appendices
April	29 30		Arrived at Havre, unloaded Transport and marched to Camp, HARFLEUR. Delousing and Bathing.	
May	2 3		Marched to HAVRE and embarked for SOUTHAMPTON. Dis-embarked at SOUTHAMPTON.	

6th. May, 1919.

Lieut. Col.,
Commanding 1/23rd. Bn. The London Regt.

www.ingramcontent.com/pod-product-compliance
Lightning Source LLC
Chambersburg PA
CBHW081527160426
43191CB00011B/1703